Patrice-Anne Rutledge

Sams **Teach Yourself**

LinkedIn®

in **10 Minutes**

800 East 96th Street, Indianapolis, Indiana 46240

Sams Teach Yourself LinkedIn® in 10 Minutes

ISBN-13: 978-0-672-33085-8
ISBN-10: 0-672-33085-7

Library of Congress Cataloging-in-Publication data is on file.

Printed in the United States of America

First printing August 2009

Trademarks

Warning and Disclaimer

Bulk Sales

Sams Publishing offers excellent discounts on this book when ordered in quantity for bulk purchases or special sales. For more information, please contact

U.S. Corporate and Government Sales

1-800-382-3419

corpsales@pearsontechgroup.com

For sales outside of the U.S., please contact

International Sales

international@pearson.com

Associate Publisher
Greg Wiegand

Acquisitions Editor
Michelle Newcomb

Development Editor
Wordsmithery LLC

Managing Editor
Patrick Kanouse

Project Editor
Seth Kerney

Copy Editor
BoxTwelve

Indexer
Ken Johnson

Proofreader
Apostrophe Editing Services

Technical Editor
Vince Averello

Publishing Coordinator
Cindy Teeters

Book Designer
Anne Jones

Composition
Bronkella Publishing, LLC

Contents

About the Author

Patrice-Anne Rutledge is a bestselling author of 27 books and a business technology expert who has been featured on CNN.com, AOL, CareerBuilder, Inc.com, Fox News, MSN, and other media outlets around the world. She specializes in teaching others to maximize the power of new technologies such as social media and online collaboration to promote their businesses and careers. Patrice is a long-time LinkedIn member and social networking advocate who uses LinkedIn to develop her business, find clients, recruit staff, and much more. Her other books include *The Truth About Profiting from Social Networking* from Pearson/FT Press. She can be reached through her website at www.patricerutledge.com.

Dedication

To my family, with thanks for their ongoing support and encouragement.

Acknowledgments

Special thanks to Michelle Newcomb, Charlotte Kughen, Vince Averello, Patrick Kanouse, Jeff Riley, and Seth Kerney for their feedback, suggestions, and attention to detail.

We Want to Hear from You!

As the reader of this book, *you* are our most important critic and commentator. We value your opinion and want to know what we're doing right, what we could do better, what areas you'd like to see us publish in, and any other words of wisdom you're willing to pass our way.

You can email or write me directly to let me know what you did or didn't like about this book—as well as what we can do to make our books stronger.

Please note that I cannot help you with technical problems related to the topic of this book, and that due to the high volume of mail I receive, I might not be able to reply to every message.

When you write, please be sure to include this book's title and author as well as your name and phone or email address. I will carefully review your comments and share them with the author and editors who worked on the book.

Email: feedback@samspublishing.com

Mail: Greg Wiegand
          Associate Publisher
          Sams Publishing
          800 East 96th Street
          Indianapolis, IN 46240 USA

Reader Services

Visit our website and register this book at www.informit.com/title/ 9780672330858 for convenient access to any updates, downloads, or errata that might be available for this book.

Introduction

Although professionals have always acknowledged the value of networking, today's economic climate makes developing a solid network even more critical. LinkedIn, the leading social networking site for professionals, is the ideal tool for maximizing the potential of an online network. LinkedIn has more than 40 million members worldwide, including executives from all Fortune 500 firms and President Barack Obama. A new member joins approximately every second.

It's clear that today's technology has forever changed the way people find a job, promote their business, foster strategic partnerships, and develop their professional networks. But technology is just the enabler. The fundamental concepts of professional networking remain the same both online and off. Building relationships through mutual connections and trust is the foundation of success on LinkedIn just as it is in the real world.

Sams Teach Yourself LinkedIn in 10 Minutes is designed to get you up and running on LinkedIn as quickly as possible. This book focuses on standard LinkedIn functionality. LinkedIn rolls out beta functionality and new features on a regular basis, so the features available to you might vary at any given time. The companion website to this book will help keep you updated on what's new with LinkedIn. For now, turn to Lesson 1, "Introducing LinkedIn," to get started with this powerful networking tool.

Who Is This Book For?

This book is for you if...

▶ You're new to LinkedIn and want to become productive as quickly as possible.

▶ You want to find a job or promote your business online, taking advantage of all that social networking has to offer.

▶ You want to become productive on LinkedIn as quickly as possible and are short on time.

Companion Websites

This book has a companion website online at
http://www.patricerutledge.com/books/linkedin.

Additional information is located at http://www.informit.com/store/
product.aspx?isbn=0672330857. Here you can find additional lessons and
articles, including information about recruiting job candidates, working
with company profiles, advertising on LinkedIn, and using LinkedIn on
your mobile device.

Conventions Used in This Book

The Teach Yourself series has several unique elements that help you as
you learn more about LinkedIn. These include

> NOTE
> A note presents interesting pieces of information related to the
> discussion.

> TIP
> A tip offers advice or teaches an easier way to do something.

> CAUTION
> A caution advises you about potential problems and helps you steer
> clear of disaster.

> PLAIN ENGLISH
> Plain English sidebars provide clear definitions of new, essential
> terms.

LESSON 1

Introducing LinkedIn

In this lesson, you'll learn the basics of LinkedIn and develop a strategy for success with this popular social networking site.

Understanding What LinkedIn Can Do for You

LinkedIn (www.linkedin.com) is the world's leading social networking site for business, with profiles of more than 40 million professionals around the world. LinkedIn is also rapidly expanding: A new member joins approximately every second. The site is extremely active with recruiters from recruiting firms as well as from major companies such as Microsoft, eBay, and L'Oréal, which makes it a prime hunting ground for job seekers.

Everyone from top CEOs to President Barack Obama has a LinkedIn profile. If you want to network for business on just one social networking site, LinkedIn is the site to choose.

> **NOTE: LinkedIn History**
> LinkedIn was founded in May 2003 when the five company founders invited 300 of their closest business contacts to join. By the end of that first year, LinkedIn had reached 81,000 members.

With LinkedIn, you can

- ▶ Create a profile that helps achieve your professional goals
- ▶ Develop and manage a network of professional contacts
- ▶ Reconnect with former colleagues and classmates

- ▶ Find jobs, consulting opportunities, and clients
- ▶ Recruit job candidates
- ▶ Request and give professional recommendations
- ▶ Find and give answers to compelling business questions
- ▶ Join groups to discuss issues with like-minded individuals
- ▶ Establish your credibility as an expert in your field
- ▶ Conduct marketing research
- ▶ Promote your services as a LinkedIn service provider
- ▶ Advertise your business

> **TIP: Focus on Strategy, Not Filling Out Forms**
> At first glance, LinkedIn appears deceptively simple. Its true power, however, comes from employing the strategic best practices of online networking, not on your ability to enter your professional data in a form.

The key to success on LinkedIn is to establish clear goals and ensure that all your actions on the site work to achieve these goals.

For example, if your goal is to find a job on LinkedIn, you want to create a strong profile with keywords that attract recruiters. You also want to develop a solid network of professional contacts in your industry—the type of people who might hire you or who might provide relevant job leads.

On the other hand, if your goal is to find business leads and develop your platform as an expert in your field, you could use a different approach. A strong profile and network are still important, but you might also want to participate in LinkedIn Answers and LinkedIn Groups to promote your expertise among LinkedIn's 40 million members.

Before establishing your goals, however, you need to understand the unwritten rules of LinkedIn. LinkedIn's focus is on developing a mutually beneficial online business network. With LinkedIn, you can stay in touch with your existing contacts and connect with other professionals who share your goals and interests. LinkedIn is not the place to amass thousands of "followers," engage in heavy sales tactics, or send spam-like communications. Keeping these "rules" in mind will help you develop a LinkedIn strategy that generates positive results in your professional career.

Understanding LinkedIn Account Types

LinkedIn offers several account types, including a free personal account and three types of premium accounts. All accounts offer the ability to create a professional profile, develop a network of contacts, search for jobs and people, receive unlimited InMail and requests for introductions, participate in groups, and participate in LinkedIn Answers.

PLAIN ENGLISH: **InMail**

An InMail is a private message from a LinkedIn member who is not your connection. Although you can receive InMail free if you indicate that you are open to receiving InMail messages, you cannot send InMail unless you pay for that particular service. InMail is a paid service because messages you send via InMail are far less likely to be confused for spam. Keep in mind, however, that InMail isn't the same as the free messages you are able to exchange with your connections after you have already made a connection.

PLAIN ENGLISH: **Introduction**

A LinkedIn introduction provides a way to reach out to people who are connected to your connections. By requesting an introduction through someone you already know, that person can introduce you to the person you're trying to reach. For example, one of your connections might be connected to a hiring manager at a company you want to work for. Requesting an introduction to this hiring manager is a much better way to find a job than just sending a resume along with hundreds of other people.

See Lesson 6, "Communicating with Other LinkedIn Members," for more information about messages, InMail, and introductions.

With a free Personal Account, you can request a maximum of five introductions at one time, view 100 results per search, and save a maximum of three searches with weekly email alerts.

> **NOTE: LinkedIn Is a Powerful Search Tool**
>
> You can perform and save targeted searches for people, jobs, companies, and other LinkedIn content. See Lesson 7, "Searching on LinkedIn," for more information about LinkedIn search capabilities.

LinkedIn's free account offers so many powerful features that it should suit the needs of most users. Unless you specifically need a premium feature, try out the free account first before making the decision to upgrade.

Exploring LinkedIn Premium Accounts

Premium accounts offer you the ability to contact more people who aren't connected to you and are ideally suited to recruiters or people using LinkedIn as a business development tool.

LinkedIn's premium accounts enable you to

- Perform unlimited one-click reference searches
- Receive an OpenLink Network membership
- Send unlimited OpenLink messages
- Receive LinkedIn customer service responses within one business day

PLAIN ENGLISH: **OpenLink Network**

The OpenLink Network is a LinkedIn premium feature that enables network members to contact each other without incurring additional fees.

Your choice of the specific premium account that's right for you depends on your needs for InMail, introductions, and searches.

The **Business Account** costs US $24.95 per month. With this account, you can

▶ Send three InMails per month, rolling over a maximum of nine unused InMails to the next month

▶ Save five searches and receive weekly alerts on each

▶ Maintain 15 pending introductions at one time

▶ View 300 results per search

The **Business Plus Account** is priced at US $49.95 per month. With this account, you can

▶ Send 10 InMails per month, rolling over a maximum of 30 unused InMails to the next month

▶ Save 7 searches and receive weekly alerts on each

▶ Maintain 25 pending introductions at one time

▶ View 500 results per search

The **Pro** account, at $499.95 per month, might interest power users. Pro users can

▶ Send 50 InMails per month, rolling over a maximum of 150 unused InMails to the next month

▶ Save 10 searches and receive daily alerts on each

▶ Maintain 40 pending introductions at one time

▶ View 700 results per search

NOTE: **Get More with LinkedIn Talent Advantage**
If you need a higher volume of InMails and introductions than the available premium accounts offer, consider signing up for LinkedIn Talent Advantage (talent.linkedin.com), a suite of power solutions for recruiters.

Creating a LinkedIn Account

Signing up for a LinkedIn account is a simple, straightforward task. Figure 1.1 shows the welcome screen that greets you the first time you visit LinkedIn (www.linkedin.com).

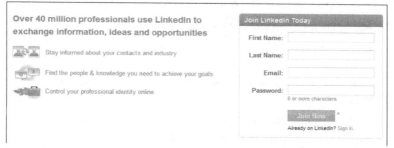

FIGURE 1.1   You can quickly sign up for your own free account from LinkedIn's home page.

To create your own LinkedIn account, follow these steps:

1. In the Join LinkedIn Today box, enter your first and last names, email address, and a password. Be sure to create a strong password. A password that contains a combination of uppercase and lowercase letters, numbers, and symbols provides the most protection.

TIP: **Choose the Right Email Address**

LinkedIn offers privacy controls to protect your business email address. Entering the email address that most of your business contacts use to communicate with you yields the best results when others try to connect with you by email on LinkedIn.

2. Click the Join Now button. The Your Account Has Been Created page appears, shown in Figure 1.2.

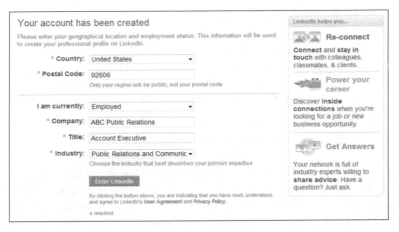

FIGURE 1.2   Enter your basic data to get started on LinkedIn.

3. Enter your Country and Postal Code. Note that LinkedIn will display only your geographic region, such as San Francisco Bay Area, and not your actual postal code or city on your profile.

4. In the I Am Currently field, select your employment status from the options available. For example, you can specify that you're employed, a business owner, looking for work, and so forth.

5. Enter your Company. As you start typing, LinkedIn locates potential company matches from existing profiles. Choosing from an existing entry helps ensure that you and your colleagues are correctly linked by company.

6. Select the Industry that best describes your professional expertise from a list of more than 100 options. These options range from popular professions (Accounting, Banking, Computer Software, Internet, Real Estate, and Marketing) to the more obscure (Dairy, Gambling & Casinos, Fishery, and Think Tanks).

7. Click the Enter LinkedIn button to open your LinkedIn home page. A sample home page is shown in Figure 1.3.

At the top of your home page, LinkedIn prompts you to confirm your email address. As a security measure, LinkedIn sends a confirmation message to the email address you entered when you signed up for an account. Click the link in this message to confirm. This ensures that the person who actually owns an email account signed up for LinkedIn and not someone else.

> TIP: **Your Confirmation May Be in Your Junk Mail Folder**
>
> If you don't receive a confirmation message from LinkedIn, check your spam or junk mail folder. Alternatively, click the Request Another One link in the Confirm Your Email Address box on your LinkedIn home page to resend the confirmation.

FIGURE 1.3 Your home page is your main LinkedIn dashboard.

When you first sign up, the Build Your Network box (refer to Figure 1.3) on your home page encourages you to start connecting with your existing contacts. However, I recommend that you create your profile before completing this step. Why? Because when your contacts receive your connection request, you want them to view a complete profile, not an empty one.

See Lesson 2, "Creating Your Profile," for more information on creating your own profile. See Lesson 3, "Adding and Managing Connections," for more information on building your LinkedIn network.

Now that you have a LinkedIn account, click the Sign In link whenever you visit the site to log on again with your primary email address and password. If you forget your password, click the Forgot Password? link on the Sign in to LinkedIn page to request a new one. If you always use the same computer to access LinkedIn, such as a home computer, you can remain logged in for up to 24 hours as a convenience.

When you first sign up for LinkedIn, you receive a personal account. To upgrade a personal account to a premium account, click the Upgrade Your Account link on the bottom navigation menu.

Exploring the LinkedIn Home Page

Your home page appears when you log on to LinkedIn. Figure 1.3 shows a sample home page, which is the dashboard of your LinkedIn activity. The content on your home page is dynamic and is unique to your LinkedIn actions, network, and account settings.

When you first create a LinkedIn account, your home page displays the Build Your Network box. After you create a profile and develop a network of more than 20 connections, however, LinkedIn allows you to close this box by clicking the Close (x) button that appears in the upper-right corner.

The center column of your home page includes the following content:

▶ **Inbox**. Displays a preview of your inbox with links to the five most recent unread messages. If you don't have at least five unread messages, the preview displays the number of unread messages that are available. See Lesson 6 for more information about your inbox.

▶ **Network Updates**. Displays your current status and a text box for updating your status. See Lesson 5, "Managing and Updating Your Profile," for more information about status updates. This section also lists recent updates from your connections.

TIP: **View Your Network Updates as an RSS Feed**

Click the orange feed icon next to the Network Updates heading to open the LinkedIn RSS Feeds page where you can subscribe to your LinkedIn network updates and read them in a feed reader. See Lesson 4, "Customizing Your LinkedIn Settings," for more information on RSS and feeds.

▶ **Group Updates**. Displays recent group updates, including information about the groups your connections joined and comments and recommendations from fellow group members.

▶ **News**. Displays recent news articles about your company, competitors, and industry. You can also participate in discussions with your colleagues about news articles, recommend news to your colleagues, share news with your connections, or submit your own articles.

NOTE: **Where Is the News Section?**

The News section appears on your home page only if news is available for your current employer. If you're self-employed or work for a small company, this section might not appear on your home page.

▶ **Just Joined LinkedIn**. Displays links to new colleagues and classmates who have joined LinkedIn recently.

TIP: **Customize Your Home Page for Easier Viewing**

To customize the network updates that appear on your home page, click the Account & Settings link in the top navigation menu and click the Network Updates link to open the Network Updates page.

The right column of your home page displays

▶ A list of three people you might know based on your existing connections. You can click the Invite link to the right of their name to send an invitation to connect. If you haven't added any connections yet on LinkedIn, this option won't appear.

▶ An advertisement.

▶ The Who's Viewed My Profile? box. Click the See More link to learn more about the people who have viewed your profile. If you haven't created a profile yet or no one has viewed your profile, this option won't appear.

▶ Boxes for LinkedIn applications and features, such as Events, LinkedIn Answers, Jobs, and Amazon Reading List recommendations. LinkedIn uses the information from your profile to determine relevant content to display. For example, if you select Marketing as your industry, the content displayed should be useful to a marketing professional. See Lesson 13, "Using LinkedIn Applications," to learn more about LinkedIn applications.

> TIP: **Customize the Applications that Appear on Your Home Page**
>
> To remove a box that displays in this column, click the X button in the upper-right corner of the box. Some boxes include an Edit link that you can click to customize the data that appears. To add application boxes, click the Add an Application button at the bottom of the column to select from the available options.

Navigating LinkedIn

Navigating LinkedIn is a straightforward process once you understand its navigational structure. LinkedIn pages display three navigation menus: one at the top of the page, one at the bottom of the page, and one on the left side of the page.

FIGURE 1.4 LinkedIn's top navigation menu provides links to common tasks.

The top navigation menu, shown in Figure 1.4, includes the following links

- ▶ **People**. Perform an advanced people search or reference search.

- ▶ **Jobs**. Perform an advanced job search or manage job postings.

- ▶ **Answers**. Ask or answer questions from other LinkedIn members.

- ▶ **Companies**. Search companies or service providers.

- ▶ **Account & Settings**. Customize the way you use LinkedIn.

- ▶ **Help**. Search LinkedIn online help.

- ▶ **Sign Out**. Log off LinkedIn.

- ▶ **Language**. Specify your language of preference. Options include English, French, German, and Spanish.

- ▶ **Search**. Select a search type from the drop-down list (Search People is the default setting), enter a search term in the text box, and click the Search button to perform the search. Click the Advanced link for advanced search options.

On the left side of the LinkedIn screen is a collapsible menu with other common navigation options, shown in Figure 1.5.

Click the plus (+) sign to expand the following options:

- ▶ **Home**. Return to the LinkedIn home page.

- ▶ **Groups**. View your groups, view a group directory, or create a group.

- ▶ **Profile**. Edit or view your profile.

- ▶ **Contacts**. Manage, add, and import connections.

- ▶ **Inbox**. View, send, and archive LinkedIn messages.

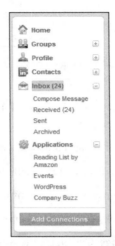

FIGURE 1.5   Be sure to click the plus (+) sign to expand the options on this navigation menu.

> ▶ **Applications**. Add, manage, or remove LinkedIn applications. By default, the Reading List by Amazon and Events applications appear.

The Add Connections button appears below the left navigation menu. Click this button to send invitations to potential LinkedIn connections.

The bottom of the LinkedIn screen links to additional menu options, including LinkedIn company information, LinkedIn tools, and premium features.

You'll learn more about these and other LinkedIn features later in this book.

Summary

In this first lesson, you learned about the many features LinkedIn offers, strategies for using the site, how to sign up for an account, and basic navigational tools. Next, it's time to create your profile.

LESSON 2

Creating Your Profile

In this lesson, you'll learn how to create a LinkedIn profile that generates results.

Viewing a LinkedIn Profile

Profiles form the foundation of LinkedIn. Your profile is your LinkedIn calling card, providing a quick snapshot of your professional background and experience.

Figure 2.1 illustrates a sample LinkedIn profile.

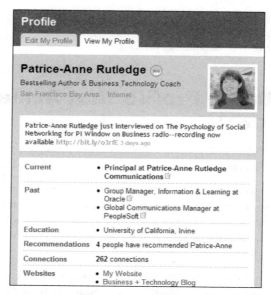

FIGURE 2.1   A solid profile generates positive results on LinkedIn.

A profile can include the following:

- ▶ A summary of your professional experience and specialties
- ▶ Your photo
- ▶ Your current status with comments from your network
- ▶ A list of the positions you've held and your major accomplishments at each
- ▶ A list of the educational institutions you've attended and your major accomplishments at each
- ▶ Professional recommendations
- ▶ Data from LinkedIn applications such as your blog feed, Amazon reading list, shared presentations, and more
- ▶ A list of your LinkedIn connections
- ▶ Information about your interests, association memberships, honors, and awards
- ▶ Your contact settings
- ▶ A list of your opportunity preferences

Creating a Profile That Achieves Your Goals

Before you create your profile, you need to think strategically about what you want to accomplish. Here are some tips for creating a quality profile:

- ▶ Set goals for what you want to achieve on LinkedIn. Are you looking for a job? Do you want to develop your business and find new clients? Are you a recruiter seeking passive job candidates? Make sure that everything you include in your profile works toward achieving that goal.
- ▶ Make a list of keywords that relate to your experience, education, certifications, profession, and industry. Every industry has

its buzzwords, and you need to include these if they're terms a recruiter or potential client would search for. For example, an IT professional may include keywords such as Java, Oracle, SAP, or AJAX. A project manager might select PMP, PMI, UML, SDLC, or Six Sigma. A public relations professional, on the other hand, could choose PRSA, APR, or social media.

▶ Have your current resume handy for easier profile completion. You can refer to it for any necessary dates or other data you might have forgotten.

CAUTION: **A Profile Isn't a Resume**

Remember, though, that a profile shouldn't duplicate your resume. A profile is a strategic summary of your professional background designed to achieve specific goals.

TIP: **Use the Box.net Files Application to Attach Documents to Your Profile**

If you really do want to include a resume on your LinkedIn profile, consider adding the Box.net Files application. With Box.net, you can share files such as PDF or Word documents on your profile. See Lesson 13, "Using LinkedIn Applications," for more information about Box.net.

▶ Check for spelling and grammar errors. Nothing detracts more from a good profile than numerous typos.

▶ Remember that most people just scan your profile. You need to capture their attention quickly and not overwhelm them with unnecessary details that detract from your goals.

▶ Keep it professional. A few personal details such as your interests help humanize your profile, but too much emphasis on outside activities also detracts from your professional goals.

CAUTION: **Protect Your Privacy**

Keep privacy issues in mind as you complete your profile. Only enter data that you're willing to share publicly.

Understanding Profile Completeness

To view your own profile, click the Edit My Profile link on the expanded left navigation menu. The Profile page opens with the Edit My Profile tab selected, shown in Figure 2.2.

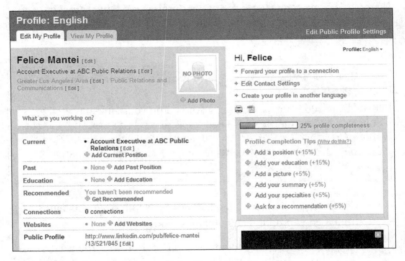

FIGURE 2.2   Create your profile on the Edit My Profile page.

On the right side of your screen, you'll see a box that displays your profile completeness. It should be about 25 percent at this point, just for signing up for a LinkedIn account. This box displays a list of the additional percentage points you receive for completing specific tasks.

NOTE: **How LinkedIn Calculates Completeness**

You might notice that adding the listed percentages to your existing 25 percent still doesn't amount to 100 percent. That's because you need at least two past positions and three recommendations to achieve profile completeness.

To achieve a profile completeness of 100 percent, you need to complete the following items:

▶ Your current position

▶ At least two past positions

▶ Your education

▶ A profile summary

▶ A profile photo

▶ Your specialties

▶ At least three recommendations

Having a complete profile encourages people to network with you. In fact, LinkedIn indicates that users with complete profiles are 40 times more likely to receive opportunities than those with incomplete profiles.

TIP: **Move Beyond What a Computer Thinks Is Complete**

Just filling out the required fields to achieve 100 percent completion doesn't guarantee success. You also need the right profile content. A few words in a field may count toward a computer's view of "completeness," but it won't be effective if your profile still contains minimal information.

Entering Basic Profile Information

Now that you have a plan for creating a solid profile, it's time to get started entering data. To create your profile, click the Edit My Profile link on the expanded left navigation menu.

The Edit My Profile tab displays your name, title, company, location, and industry based on the data you entered when you signed up. Click the Edit link next to any entry you want to change; this opens the Basic Information page.

The Basic Information page also includes several new fields. These include

- ▶ **Former/Maiden Name.** If you've changed your name at any point during your career, it could be difficult for former classmates or colleagues to find you. Entering your Former/Maiden Name makes it easier when people search for your former name.

- ▶ **Display Name.** By default, LinkedIn displays your full name. If you have strong privacy concerns, you can choose to display only your first name and last initial to anyone other than your own connections.

- ▶ **Professional Headline.** LinkedIn uses a combination of your title and company name as your Professional Headline, which should be sufficient for most people. You may want to customize this, however, if you're seeking work, are self-employed, or maintain more than one job. Some people include targeted keywords, professional certifications, or degrees in their professional headlines.

  Some examples:

  - ▶ PMP-certified IT Project Manager Seeking New Opportunities

  - ▶ Bestselling Author, Coach, and Business Consultant

  - ▶ Public Relations Executive, MBA, APR, Fellow PRSA

Make your changes, then click the Save Changes button to return to the Edit My Profile tab.

Adding Positions

Although you already entered your current job title and company when you created your LinkedIn account, you'll want to expand on that basic information. To do so, click the Edit link next to your current position on the Edit My Profile tab to open the Edit Position page, shown in Figure 2.3.

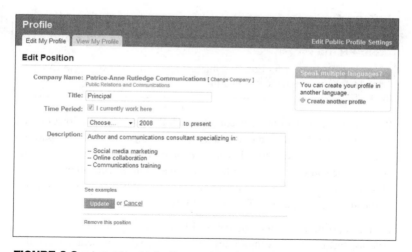

FIGURE 2.3 Let other LinkedIn members know about your professional success.

Enter a brief description of your current position, make any additional changes to the information you previously entered, and click the Update button.

Here are a few tips on what to include in the Description field:

▶ Use keywords. Think of the terms people would search for and use them in your description. For example, if you work in IT, mention actual technologies rather than vague generalizations.

▶ Emphasize accomplishments over job duties. For example, rather than say that you're responsible for sales, focus on your sales achievements and awards.

▶ Be brief. The Description field is a summary, not a detailed resume.

▶ Keep your goals in mind. If you want to attract recruiters, think about what would interest them in a potential candidate. If you're seeking clients for your business, focus on what would make them want to hire you.

NOTE: **Remove Positions You No Longer Want to Appear on Your Profile**

Click the Remove This Position link on the Edit Position page to delete that position from LinkedIn.

If you hold more than one current job, click the Add Current Position link on the Edit My Profile tab to add another current position. This is particularly useful for self-employed or independent professionals who have several income sources. For example, if you're an author, consultant, and blogger, you could choose to combine these activities under one position or create a unique position for each activity.

Add past positions by clicking the Add Past Position link on that tab. Adding past positions is important because it provides a clearer view of your background and makes it easier to connect with your former colleagues at previous companies.

> TIP: **Focus on the Last 10 to 15 Years of Employment**
> If you have extensive experience, it's a good idea to focus only on the past 10 to 15 years of your work life unless an early position in your career is very relevant to your current goals.

Adding Educational Information

Next, you'll add information about your educational background. LinkedIn uses this information to help you connect easily with former classmates.

Consider the following best practices when choosing what educational information to enter:

- ▶ Include colleges and universities from which you received a degree.

- ▶ Include **relevant** certificates and continuing education course-work. For example, if you're looking for a job in a new field and have completed a related certificate, you should include this information.

- ▶ Don't include every continuing education course or seminar you've ever taken. It's important to be strategic, not prolific.

- ▶ Don't include your high school information unless you're still in college, are a recent graduate, or specifically want to reconnect with high school classmates.

To enter educational information, follow these steps:

1. Click the Add Education link on the Edit My Profile tab. The Add Education page opens, shown in Figure 2.4.

2. Select your Country (and State, if you're in the United States).

3. Select your School Name from the drop-down list that displays. If you can't find your school in the list, scroll down to the end and select Other. You can then enter your school name manually in the Type School Name field.

FIGURE 2.4   Provide a summary of your educational accomplishments.

4. Enter your Degree, such as BA, BS, or MBA.

5. Enter your Field(s) of Study. This can be your major, an area of concentration, or the name of a certificate.

6. In the Dates Attended fields, enter the years you attended. If you're still a student, enter your anticipated year of graduation in the second field.

NOTE: **Deciding Whether to Include Graduation Years**

The decision whether to include your year of graduation is a personal choice for many experienced professionals. LinkedIn doesn't require you to list the year you graduated; this is an optional field. Keep in mind, however, that LinkedIn won't be able to automatically search for your former classmates if you omit your graduation year. You would need to perform a manual search for former classmates.

---

7. List relevant activities in the Activities and Societies field. This might include honors, study abroad, and any extracurricular activities.

8. Add any Additional Notes about your educational experience.

9. Click the Save Changes button to return to the Edit My Profile tab.

NOTE: **Enter Only Relevant Information**

You don't need to complete all the fields on the Add Education page to provide an accurate picture of your educational background. For example, details about your participation with the ski club or theater groups won't add real value to your LinkedIn profile. Entering the most pertinent data ensures that people who read your profile focus on what's relevant.

The next section on the Edit My Profile tab, Recommended, encourages you to request professional recommendations. My recommendation, however, is for you to first complete your profile and then add connections before requesting recommendations. See Lesson 10, "Requesting and Providing Recommendations" for more information about LinkedIn recommendations.

Adding Websites and Other Additional Information

To list websites on your LinkedIn profile—as well as add other information about your interests and achievements—follow these steps:

1. Click the Add Websites link on the Edit My Profile tab. The Additional Information page opens, shown in Figure 2.5.

2. From the Websites drop-down list, select the type of link you want to add. Options include My Website, My Company, My Blog, My RSS Feed, My Portfolio, or Other. If you select Other, a text box appears in which you can enter the name of your choice.

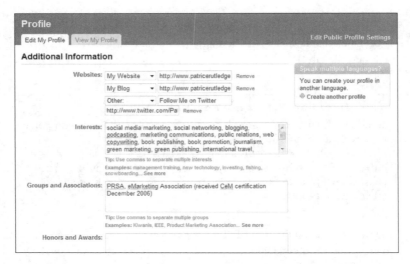

FIGURE 2.5   Add links to your website or blog on your LinkedIn profile.

TIP: **Gain Name Recognition for Your Sites**

You can use the Other option to gain name recognition for your site or blog. For example, if you have a blog called Project Management Best Practices, you might prefer to create a link with that name rather than using the generic "My Website" or "My Blog." In addition, you can use this field to link to Twitter or other social sites.

---

3. Enter the complete URL of the site you want to link to, such as http://www.patricerutledge.com.

NOTE: **You Can List a Maximum of Three Sites**

To avoid clutter and prevent link spam, you can enter only three websites on your LinkedIn profile. If you have more than three sites to consider, think carefully about which sites would generate the most interest on a business networking site such as LinkedIn.

4. In the Interests text box, enter a list of your professional and per-sonal interests. Be sure to use commas to separate interests so this content is searchable. Each interest becomes a link on your actual profile that you can click to search for others who share your interests. Again, think about meaningful keywords for this section rather than lengthy descriptions.

5. List the Groups and Associations to which you belong. Use commas to separate this information as well because the terms also become searchable links on your profile.

6. List any Honors and Awards you've received.

7. Click the Save Changes button to update your profile and return to the Edit My Profile page.

Customizing Your Public Profile

LinkedIn makes a public version of your profile available to all web users, regardless of whether they're LinkedIn members or connected to you. When someone searches your name on Google or Yahoo!, for example, the public version of your profile appears in search results. Although a public profile is a great way to promote your career and gain visibility, it isn't for everyone. Don't worry. You have control over exactly what others can view on your profile. You can even hide your profile from public view if you choose.

By default, your public LinkedIn URL looks something like this: http://www.linkedin.com/pub/13/521/845. The numbers in this URL address aren't very user-friendly, however, so you'll want to customize your public profile URL to something easier to remember such as www.linkedin.com/in/patriceannerutledge.

To do so, follow these steps:

1. On the Edit My Profile tab, click the Edit link to the right of your Public Profile URL. The Public Profile page opens, as shown in Figure 2.6.

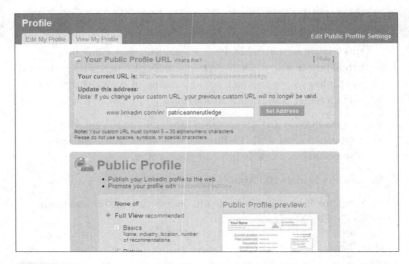

FIGURE 2.6   Create a user-friendly URL for your LinkedIn public profile.

2. Enter the custom URL you prefer. Using your first name and last name as one string of characters is a good choice. Spaces, symbols, and special characters aren't allowed in your URL.

3. Click the Set Address button to save your changes.

4. In the Public Profile section, clear the check box next to any fields you do not want to appear on your public profile.

TIP: **You Can Hide Your Profile from Public View**

To hide your entire profile from public view on the web, click the None option button in the Public Profile section.

---

5. Click the Save Changes button to update your public profile.

6. Click the View My Public Profile as Others See It link to preview what your public profile looks like on the web.

Adding a Profile Summary

The next section on the Edit My Profile tab asks you to enter a profile summary. This is an important step because people scanning your profile often read this section first.

To create your summary, follow these steps:

1. On the Edit My Profile tab, click the Edit link to the right of the Summary heading. The Summary page opens, shown in Figure 2.7.

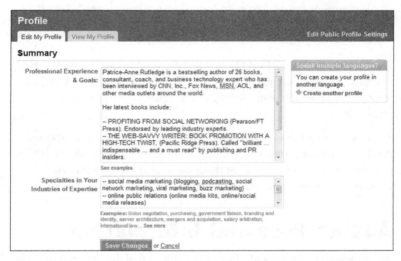

FIGURE 2.7 Provide a concise summary of your professional accomplishments.

TIP: **Review Other Profiles in Your Industry**

To get some ideas about what to include in your summary section, analyze the profiles of others in your profession or industry. Each industry has its own buzzwords and "personality," so what works for one professional might not be as appropriate for another.

2. Enter a summary of your Professional Experience & Goals. In addition to summarizing your professional experience, you can also use this field to indicate that you're looking for job opportunities (assuming you're currently unemployed), recruiting staff, accepting new clients, or seeking new business partners, for example. Be sure to keep it professional, however. This is not the place for an advertisement or sales hype.

3. List your specialties in the Specialties in Your Industries of Expertise field.

4. Click the Save Changes button to return to the Edit My Profile tab.

The next section on the Edit My Profile tab, Applications, suggests several applications you can add to your profile. See Lesson 13 for more information about the many ways you can benefit from LinkedIn applications.

The next four sections—Experience, Education, Recommended By, and Additional Information—appeared earlier on the Edit My Profile tab. You can click the Edit links in any of these sections to make additional changes, or you can continue to the next section.

Adding Personal Information

At the bottom of the Edit My Profile tab, you'll find the Personal Information section. In this section, you can enter the following data:

▶ Phone

▶ Address

▶ IM (instant message)

▶ Birthday

▶ Marital Status

If you want to add any of this information to your profile, click the Edit link to open the Personal Information page. The Birthday, Birth Year, and

Marital Status fields display a lock button next to them. Click this button to restrict visibility to only your connections or only your network.

> **CAUTION: Consider Your Personal Privacy**
>
> Entering any data in the Personal Information section is optional. Carefully consider your personal privacy before making any personal information public, even to a restricted group of people.

Specifying Contact Settings

Next, specify what types of messages you'll accept and what opportunities you're interested in. To update the Contact Settings page, shown in Figure 2.8, follow these steps:

FIGURE 2.8   Tell other LinkedIn members about your contact preferences.

1. At the bottom of the Edit My Profile page, click the Edit link next to the Contact Settings heading.

2. In the What Type Of Messages Will You Accept? field, indicate whether you'll accept both introductions and InMail or if you'll accept only introductions. See Lesson 6, "Communicating with Other LinkedIn Members," for more information about InMail and introductions.

3. In the Opportunity Preferences section, indicate the opportunities you're open to. If you're looking for a job or recruiting staff, for example, it's important to let people know this. Your options include

   ▶ Career opportunities

   ▶ Expertise requests

   ▶ Consulting offers

   ▶ Business deals

   ▶ New ventures

   ▶ Personal reference requests

   ▶ Job inquiries

   ▶ Requests to reconnect

4. Enter the advice you would give to members considering contacting you. In this text box, you can indicate that you're open to connecting with new people, you want to connect only with people you know, and so forth.

5. Click the Save Changes button to return to the Edit My Profile tab.

Adding a Profile Photo

Finally, you should add a photo to your LinkedIn profile. A photo helps bring your profile to life and sets you apart from other LinkedIn members. A professional headshot works best on your LinkedIn profile.

To upload your photo, follow these steps:

1. At the top of the Edit My Profile tab, click the Add Photo link. The Edit Photo page appears, as shown in Figure 2.9.

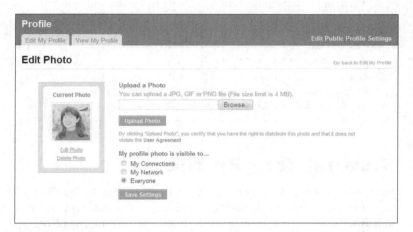

FIGURE 2.9   Let a professional photo bring your LinkedIn profile to life.

2. Click the Browse button to open the File Upload dialog box.

3. Select the photo you want to upload and click the Open button.

> NOTE: **Photo Format and Size Limits**
>
> You can upload a photo in a JPG, GIF, or PNG file format. The file cannot be larger than 4MB.

4. Click the Upload Photo button. LinkedIn shows you a preview of how your photo will appear on your profile.

5. Use LinkedIn's resizing tool to make any modifications, and click the Save Photo button to complete the upload process.

6. Indicate your photo visibility preferences. You can specify that your photo is visible to your connections, to your network, or to everyone. Note that your connections include only the people you directly connect with; your network includes the people connected to your connections.

7. Click the Save Settings button to finish the upload and return to the Edit My Profile tab.

TIP: **Easily Replace or Remove Your Photo**

If you want to replace or remove your profile photo, click the Edit link below your photo on the Edit My Profile tab. Here you can upload a new photo or click the Delete Photo link to remove your photo.

Viewing Your Profile

To preview your profile, click the View My Profile tab on the Profile page. Review all your entries carefully, checking for content accuracy as well as for grammar and spelling errors. If necessary, revise any of your entries by clicking the Edit link next to the item you want edit.

See Lesson 5 for information about keeping your profile updated, printing your profile, promoting your profile on the web, and creating a profile in another language.

Summary

In this lesson, you learned how to create a quality profile that should help you achieve your goals on LinkedIn. Next, it's time to start adding connections.

LESSON 3

Adding and Managing Connections

In this lesson, you'll learn how to develop a solid LinkedIn connection strategy, connect with other members, and manage your contacts.

Developing a Connection Strategy

After creating a strong profile, the next step in making the most of your LinkedIn experience is developing a solid network of professional connections. Before you add connections to LinkedIn, however, you should develop a connection strategy that matches your goals and networking philosophy.

> TIP: **Match Your Connection Strategy with LinkedIn Goals**
> In Lesson 1, "Introducing LinkedIn," you established goals for what you want to accomplish on LinkedIn. Be sure that your connection strategy helps you meet these goals. For example, if you're looking for a new job in a specific industry, your focus will be to connect with recruiters and other professionals in that industry. If your LinkedIn goal is to develop your business or build a platform, then you may want to connect with a broader spectrum of people.

The three most common approaches are

- ▶ Connect only with people you know. LinkedIn members who follow this approach connect only with colleagues, classmates, and associates they personally know or who their known connections recommend to them.

▶ Connect with people you know plus strategic contacts you would like to know. With this approach, you connect with people you know and also seek out strategic connections who match your networking goals.

▶ Connect with anyone and everyone. Some LinkedIn members, particularly those who want to use the site for business development purposes, are open networkers and like to connect with as many people as possible and make special efforts to connect with thousands of people.

PLAIN ENGLISH: Open Networker

An open networker is a LinkedIn member who is open to connecting with people they don't know. Several LinkedIn groups exist for open networkers, such as LION (LinkedIn Open Networker) or TopLinked. Although it's a good idea to network with new people and develop a mutually beneficial business relationship, be careful not to abuse open networking by connecting indiscriminately just to amass a very large network. Don't treat your LinkedIn network as a numbers game.

Which approach is best? There is no one right answer for everyone. LinkedIn members have their own goals as to what they hope to accomplish on the site as well as their own networking strategies and comfort levels.

To get started, consider connecting with current and former colleagues, current and former classmates, friends and other acquaintances, and fellow members of professional associations.

Who to connect with beyond these obvious contacts depends on your connection strategy and networking philosophy.

Building Your Network

When you first join LinkedIn, your home page displays the Build Your Network box, shown in Figure 3.1.

FIGURE 3.1   Building a solid network of contacts is a critical step to making the most of LinkedIn's potential.

NOTE: **Closing the Build Your Network Box**

After you create a profile and develop a network of more than 20 connections, LinkedIn allows you to close the Build Your Network box by clicking the Close (x) button that appears in the upper-right corner.

For an alternate way to access these network-building tools, click the Add Connections button on the left navigation menu.

This box offers links to four easy ways to start developing your LinkedIn network. These include

- ▶ Importing your webmail contacts from services such as Gmail, Hotmail, AOL, or Yahoo! Mail

- ▶ Importing your address book contacts from Microsoft Outlook, ACT!, Palm devices, or Apple Mail

▶ Searching for current and former colleagues by company, job title, and years of employment

▶ Searching for current and former classmates by school and years of attendance

Keep in mind that you don't need to use all these methods to develop your pool of LinkedIn connections. For example, you might not want to connect with all your webmail or address book contacts. Or your webmail account might contain personal email addresses, not the email addresses your contacts used to sign up for LinkedIn.

> NOTE: **Connect with Imported Contacts Manually**
>
> Importing your webmail or address book contacts doesn't mean they automatically become LinkedIn connections. You must still manually choose whom to connect with.

Importing Webmail Contacts

If you have an email account with a popular webmail provider (such as Windows Live Hotmail, Gmail, Yahoo! Mail, or AOL), LinkedIn can import the email addresses of your web contacts.

To import webmail contacts, follow these steps:

1. In the Build Your Network box, select your webmail provider from the available options. These include Windows Live Hotmail, Gmail, Yahoo! Mail, or AOL. If your provider isn't one of these four, select the Other option button to display a list of alternative webmail providers, including many that are from outside the United States.

> TIP: **Alternate Navigation to Import Webmail Contacts**
>
> You can also import webmail contacts by clicking the Add Connections button on the left navigation menu and then clicking the Check Webmail Contacts button.

2. Enter your User Name and Password.

3. Click the Upload Contacts button. LinkedIn imports the contacts from your webmail contact list and displays these contacts in the Imported Contacts tab, shown in Figure 3.2.

4. Select the check box to the left of each contact's name you want to invite to connect on LinkedIn.

5. Select the Add a Personal Note to Your Invitation check box to open a text box where you can personalize your connection request.

6. Click the Invite Selected Contacts button to send your invitations.

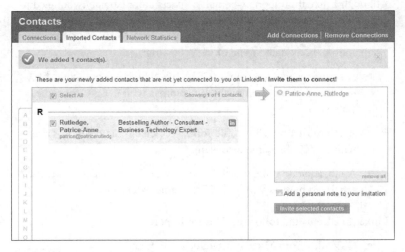

FIGURE 3.2 Select the webmail contacts you want to connect with on LinkedIn.

NOTE: **Confirm Your Email Address Before Connecting**
You can't send connection requests until you confirm your email address. If you need to request a new confirmation message from LinkedIn, click the Account & Setting link in the top navigation menu and then click the Email Addresses link. Select the email address you want to confirm and click the Send Confirmation Message button. LinkedIn sends you an email with confirmation instructions.

Your contacts will receive your connection requests and choose to accept or reject your request.

Importing Contacts from Other Email Systems

Although LinkedIn imports webmail contacts automatically, you need to export your contacts from other email systems as a separate step. To do so, follow the instructions your email system provides for exporting your email address book data to one of the following:

- ▶ A comma-separated values (CSV) file, which is a computer file in which fields are separated by commas with a .CSV filename extension

- ▶ A vCard file, which is a file format for electronic business cards with a .VCF filename extension

- ▶ A tab-separated file, which is a computer file in which fields are separated by tabs with a .TXT filename extension

LinkedIn accepts the following files for import:

- ▶ CSV files from Microsoft Outlook

- ▶ CSV or tab-separated files from Palm Desktop

- ▶ CSV files from ACT!

- ▶ vCard files from Palm Desktop

- ▶ vCard files from Mac OX X Address Book

To import a file exported from an email system, follow these steps:

1. In the Build Your Network box, click the Find button in the Address Book Contacts section. The Add Connections page appears.

> **TIP: Alternate Navigation to Import Email Contacts**
> You can also import email contacts by clicking the Add Connections button on the left navigation menu, clicking the Import Contacts tab, and clicking the Other Address Book button.

2. Click the Browse button to select the appropriate file on your computer.

3. Click the Upload Contacts File button. LinkedIn imports your file and asks you to verify the accuracy of the data you imported.

4. If your data looks accurate, click the Finish Upload button.

LinkedIn returns to the Imported Contacts tab where you can send invitations to your new contacts.

> **TIP: Verify the Accuracy of Your Uploaded Data**
> If your data doesn't look accurate, click the Cancel Upload button and start your import again.

Connecting with Current or Past Colleagues

To connect with current or past colleagues from the Build Your Network box, follow these steps:

1. Click the Find button in the Current and Past Colleagues section. The Reconnect with Past Colleagues page appears, shown in Figure 3.3.

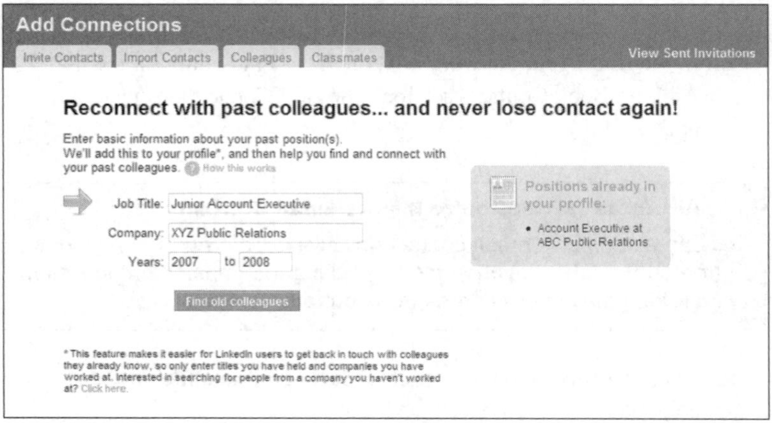

FIGURE 3.3   Connecting with your current and past colleagues is a great way to build your online network.

TIP: **Alternate Navigation to Search for Colleagues**

You can also search for colleagues by clicking the Add Connections button on the left navigation menu and selecting the Colleagues tab.

---

2. Enter your Job Title, Company, and Years of employment for any past positions. LinkedIn will also search for the current position you entered when you signed up for your account.

3. Click the Find Old Colleagues button. LinkedIn displays a list of colleagues who worked at the same companies at the same time as you.

4. Select the individuals you know.

5. Click the Send Invitations button to send connection requests to these people.

TIP: **Personalize Your Connection Request**

Select the Add a Personal Note with Your Invitation? check box to add a personalized greeting to your connection request. Personalizing your request is particularly useful when reaching out to colleagues you haven't worked with in a while.

Connecting with Former Classmates

To connect with current or former classmates from the Build Your Network box, follow these steps:

1. Click the Find button in the Former Classmates section. The Classmates page appears.

TIP: **Alternate Navigation to Search for Classmates**
You can also search for colleagues by clicking the Add Connections button on the left navigation menu and clicking the Classmates tab.

2. Click the link for the university you want to search from the list of schools from your profile.

TIP: **Search for Former Classmates from All the Schools You Attended**

If you didn't finish adding schools to your profile, click the Add Another School to Your Profile link to find classmates from additional schools.

3. View the search results and click the Invite link for the classmates you want to connect with.

TIP: **Revise Your Search Parameters for Better Results**
You can narrow or widen your search results by selecting View Graduation Year Only or View All Years Attended.

Connecting with Other LinkedIn Members

By now, you should have a good start on developing your LinkedIn network. Here are a few other suggestions for finding worthwhile connections on LinkedIn:

▶ Review the list of people your connections are connected to, which displays in their profile. It's very likely that you know some of the same people and would like to connect with them as well. View the profile of the person you want to connect with and click the Add [person's name] to Your Network link to send an invitation from the Add Connections page. For example, to connect with Felice Mantei, you would click the Add Felice to Your Network link.

▶ Search for individuals by name in the Search People box on the top navigation menu. Click the Add to Network link to the right of the person you want to connect with to open the Add Connections page. For additional search options, click the Advanced link.

▶ Search by keyword and location on the Advanced Search page to find local members of your professional associations. Click the Advanced link on the top navigation menu to access this page. For example, you could search for the keyword PRSA (for the Public Relations Society of America) and the ZIP code 92606 within a 25-mile radius to find fellow PRSA members in Orange County, California.

▶ Search for potential connections among the members of any LinkedIn groups to which you belong. The Members tab provides a list of all group members and an Invite to Connect link with which to contact them. Remember, however, not to spam fellow group members with connection invitations. Be selective in determining who you want to connect with.

See Lesson 7, "Searching on LinkedIn," for more information on searching for people.

When you click the Add to Network link from any of these options, the Add Connections page appears, shown in Figure 3.4.

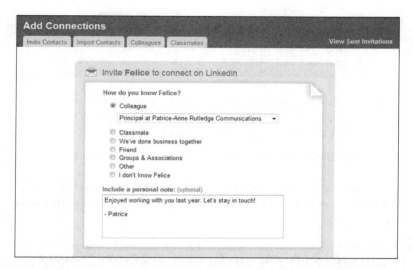

FIGURE 3.4   Specify how you know a target connection before sending an invitation.

To create a connection request on this page, follow these steps:

1. Select how you know your target connection from these options:

- ▶ **Colleague**. Select a company from the drop-down list that appears.

- ▶ **Classmate**. Select a school from the drop-down list that appears.

- ▶ **We've Done Business Together**. Select a company from the drop-down list that appears.

- ▶ **Friend**.

- ▶ **Groups & Associations**. Select a group from the drop-down list that appears.

- ▶ **Other**. Enter the person's email address.

- ▶ **I Don't Know [person's name]**.

> NOTE: **Add Connections Page Variations**
>
> If you haven't completed your profile data, you may see only a text box to enter your target connection's email address on this page.

2. Include a personal note in the text box explaining why you want to connect on LinkedIn. This is particularly important if you don't know the person you want to connect with.

3. Click the Send Invitation button to send your connection request.

See Lesson 6, "Communicating with Other LinkedIn Members," for more information on viewing the status of connection invitations and other messages.

> TIP: **Consider Other Options for Contacting People You Don't Know**
>
> Two other ways of connecting with people you don't know are to send an InMail or request an introduction. See Lesson 6 for more information on InMail and introductions.

Connecting with People Not on LinkedIn

If you discover that some of your real-world networking contacts aren't using LinkedIn yet, it's easy to invite them:

1. Click the Add Connections button at the bottom on the left navigation menu to open the Add Connections page, shown in Figure 3.5.

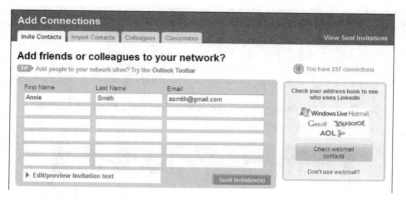

FIGURE 3.5   Invite your real-world connections to join LinkedIn.

2. Enter the First Name, Last Name, and Email address of each contact.

3. Click the Edit/Preview Invitation Text link to open a text box where you can personalize the message to your contacts. This is particularly a good idea if your contacts may not be familiar with LinkedIn and the value it provides.

4. Click the Send Invitation(s) button to send invitations.

Responding to Connection Invitations

In addition to sending invitations to connect, you might also receive invitations. To respond to an invitation, follow these steps:

1. Click the Inbox link on the left navigation menu to open your Inbox.

2. If you have several messages in your Inbox, select Invitations from the Received drop-down list. Your Inbox displays only your invitation requests. Alternatively, you can also view new invitation requests in your Inbox preview on your home page.

3. To open the request, click the subject line link. Figure 3.6 illustrates a sample request to connect.

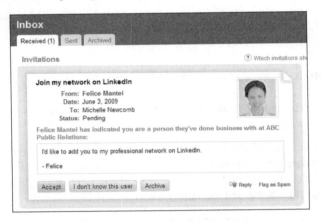

FIGURE 3.6   You must manually accept invitations to connect.

4. View the greeting from the person who wants to connect with you.

5. If you would like to open the individual's profile, click the sender's name. Reviewing a LinkedIn member's profile can help you remember more about someone you don't know well or decide whether to connect with someone you don't know at all.

6. Take one of the following actions:

   ▶ If you want to add the person to your network, click the Accept button.

   ▶ If you want to decline the invitation, click the I Don't Know This User button. LinkedIn blocks this person from inviting you again, but you can send the person an invitation in the future if you decide to do so.

▶ If you don't have time to review the invitation, click the Archive button to move the invitation to your Archived folder. You can accept or decline the invitation in the future.

▶ To send a message to the person who initiated the invitation before accepting or declining, click the Reply link. For example, you might want to ask why this person wants to connect before accepting.

▶ If you feel this invitation is spam, click the Flag as Spam link.

CAUTION: **Think Carefully Before Flagging an Invitation as Spam**

Be sure that an invitation truly is spam before flagging it. Flagging an invitation as spam is too harsh if it's a genuine request from someone you just don't want to connect with. Flagging as spam is appropriate, however, if the personalized greeting contains an overt sales pitch rather than a true connection invitation.

When you accept invitations, LinkedIn adds those members as 1st degree connections in your network. If you would like to add notes about the person and edit their contact information, use the Your Private Information About [First Name] box on their profile.

Managing Your Connections

Once you develop your LinkedIn network, you need an easy way to find and manage your existing connections. The Connections page offers several ways to do this.

Click the Connections link on the expanded left navigation menu to open the Connections page, which displays a list of your connections (see Figure 3.7).

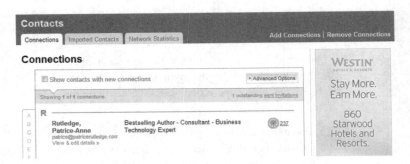

FIGURE 3.7   Find, contact, and manage your connections on the Connections page.

If you have many connections, it may be difficult to find the person you're looking for. LinkedIn offers several ways to filter your connections. You can

▶ Click the first letter of a contact's last name to display only those contacts whose names start with that letter. If you don't have any contacts for a specific letter, that letter's link isn't displayed.

▶ Select the Show Contacts with New Connections check box. Doing this lets you know which of your contacts recently connected with someone new on LinkedIn. Perhaps you know this person and would like to connect as well?

▶ Click the Advanced Options button to filter by Location or Industry.

The View & Edit Details link beneath each connection's name opens a window where you can enter more detailed information about this connection, such as a phone number or website URL. To view a connection's profile, click on that individual's name.

> NOTE: **LinkedIn Connections Beta**
>
> If you're part of the Connections Beta, you might view a different version of the Connections page. This beta version offers advanced connection tagging and filtering for easier connection management.

Removing Connections

If you decide that you no longer want to connect with someone on LinkedIn, you can remove that person as a connection:

1. Click the Connections link in the expanded left navigation menu to open the Connections page.

2. Click the Remove Connections link in the upper-right corner of the page.

3. Select the check box next to the connections you want to remove.

4. Click the Remove Connections button.

People you remove are no longer able to view any data that can be viewed only by actual connections and they also can't send you direct messages. LinkedIn, however, doesn't notify them of the fact they have been removed.

> CAUTION: **Remove Connections for the Right Reason**
>
> Be sure that a connection really warrants removal before proceeding with the removal process. For example, if a connection you don't know well is bothering you with requests, spam, or sales pitches, this person is probably a connection worth removing. Removing former colleagues or associates simply because you haven't seen them in a while or don't work with them anymore, however, can be shortsighted.

Viewing Your Network Statistics

The Network Statistics page provides some interesting statistics about your network, including your total number of connections, the number of members you can reach through an introduction, the number of new people in your network, and much more. To view these stats, click the Network Statistics link in the expanded left navigation menu.

Summary

In this lesson, you learned how to develop a connection strategy that suits your goals and started developing your own network. Next, it's time to customize your LinkedIn settings to give you the optimal online networking experience.

LESSON 4

Customizing Your LinkedIn Settings

In this lesson, you'll learn how to customize your LinkedIn profile, email, and privacy settings.

Customizing the Way You Use LinkedIn

Now that you've created a profile and connected with other LinkedIn members, it's time to customize your LinkedIn settings to optimize your experience on the site.

> TIP: **Customize for Optimal Privacy and Simplicity**
> If you're not sure which options to choose, select the ones that provide you the most privacy and simplicity while still allowing you to achieve your goals.

The Account & Settings page provides a lengthy list of options for customizing your LinkedIn experience. To access this page, shown in Figure 4.1, click the Account & Settings link on the top navigation menu.

> NOTE: **Learn More About Account Options and Upgrades**
> The top portion of the Account & Settings page describes options for upgrading your account. See Lesson 1, "Introducing LinkedIn," to learn more about LinkedIn account options and upgrades.

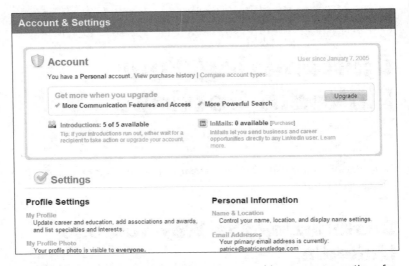

FIGURE 4.1   The Account & Settings page provides numerous options for customizing your LinkedIn experience.

> CAUTION: **Don't Skip Account Customization**
>
> The many options provided on the Account & Settings page might seem overwhelming at first, and you might be tempted to skip this step. Setting aside some time to customize the options on this page, often a one-time task, can pay off in the long run. By customizing your LinkedIn settings, you'll better protect your privacy, receive only the specific information you want, and avoid any unpleasant surprises regarding the way LinkedIn handles your personal data.

Customizing Profile Settings

To customize your profile settings, click the Account & Settings link on the top navigation menu. In the Profile Settings section of this page, you can customize the following:

▶ **My Profile**. Update and edit your profile content on the Edit Profile page.

▶ **My Profile Photo**. Upload or remove your profile photo. If you don't want everyone to view your photo, you can restrict its visibility to only your network or only your connections.

PLAIN ENGLISH: **My Connections Versus My Network**

Several of the options on this page give you the option to restrict visibility to My Connections or to My Network. My Connections refers to the LinkedIn members you connect with directly. My Network refers to the people two or three degrees away from your connections (in other words, your connections' connections). See Lesson 6, "Communicating with Other LinkedIn Members," for more information on this distinction.

▶ **Public Profile**. Specify the content you want to include in your public profile and customize your web URL.

▶ **Manage Recommendations**. Request, provide, and manage recommendations. See Lesson 10, "Requesting and Providing Recommendations" for more information about the power of LinkedIn recommendations.

▶ **Status Visibility**. Make your profile status visible to everyone or restrict it to your network or connections. See Lesson 5, "Managing and Updating Your Profile," for more information on status updates.

▶ **Member Feed Visibility**. Make your member feed visible to everyone or restrict it to your network or connections. For maximum privacy, you can choose to not display your member feed.

PLAIN ENGLISH: **Member Feed**

Your member feed refers to the network updates that appear on your home page and the home page of your connections.

Customizing Email Notification Settings

LinkedIn enables you to make extensive customizations to the way you handle email notification of various actions and activities. To customize your email notification settings, click the Account & Settings link on the top navigation menu. The Account & Settings page appears. The Email Notification Settings section of this page lets you customize your contact settings, the way you receive messages, and the invitations you receive.

To customize your contact settings, such as the way you handle InMail and introductions, click the Contact Settings link. See Lesson 2, "Creating Your Profile," for more information on contact settings.

To customize how you receive messages on LinkedIn, click the Receiving Messages link. The Receiving Messages page appears, shown in Figure 4.2.

You have four choices on the way you receive messages:

▶ **Individual Email**. LinkedIn sends an email to your primary email address as soon as the action takes place.

▶ **Daily Digest Email**. LinkedIn sends one bundled email notification per day.

▶ **Weekly Digest Email**. LinkedIn sends one bundled email notification per week.

▶ **No Email**. LinkedIn sends no email. You need to go to the website to read messages and notifications.

> NOTE: **How LinkedIn Handles Bundled Notifications**
> With bundled notifications, you don't receive a notification if there is no activity.

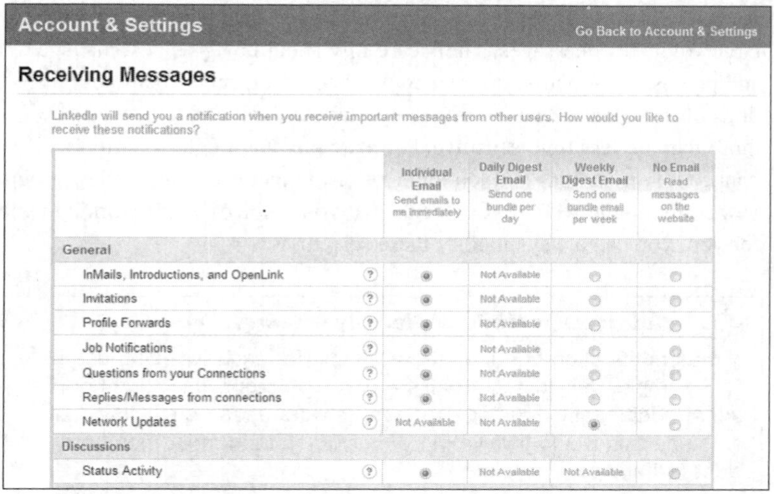

Account & Settings				Go Back to Account & Settings
Receiving Messages				
LinkedIn will send you a notification when you receive important messages from other users. How would you like to receive these notifications?				
	Individual Email Send emails to me immediately	Daily Digest Email Send one bundle per day	Weekly Digest Email Send one bundle email per week	No Email Read messages on the website
General				
InMails, Introductions, and OpenLink ⑦	◉	Not Available	○	○
Invitations ⑦	◉	Not Available	○	○
Profile Forwards ⑦	◉	Not Available	○	○
Job Notifications ⑦	◉	Not Available	○	○
Questions from your Connections ⑦	◉	Not Available	○	○
Replies/Messages from connections ⑦	◉	Not Available	○	○
Network Updates ⑦	Not Available	Not Available	◉	○
Discussions				
Status Activity ⑦	◉	Not Available	Not Available	○

FIGURE 4.2   LinkedIn enables you to provide specific instructions on its delivery of email messages.

You can further customize your notifications based on message type such as InMails, introductions, OpenLink messages, invitations to connect, status updates, group updates, and so forth.

> Replies and messages from your connections
>
> Network updates about your connections' LinkedIn activities
>
> Status activity updates such as comments on your status
>
> Invitations to join groups
>
> Group digest email by individual group

As you expand your network on LinkedIn, you could potentially receive a large volume of messages. Think carefully about how you best manage and process information. Many people choose to receive email notifications of the updates that are most important to them and review online those that are less time-sensitive. For example, you might want to receive connection invitations and job notifications immediately, but review group news only on the web. If you decide that your choices aren't working well for you, you can always modify these selections.

NOTE: **Notification Methods Vary by Message Type**

Not all notification methods are available for each type of message. For example, daily digest emails are available only for group notifications. Additionally, you can't receive network updates by individual email as this would involve more messages than most members want to handle.

Finally, you can customize which connection invitations you receive by clicking the Invitation Filtering link. By default, you receive all invitations, but you can choose to receive invitations only from those who know your email address or those who are in your Imported Contacts list. Keep in mind, however, that restricting your invitations could block an invitation from someone you might actually want to connect with.

Customizing Your Home Page Settings

Network updates on your home page give you a quick snapshot of your connections' activities on LinkedIn. Although it's good to keep up with the latest news in your network, you might find that some network updates are of more interest to you than others are. See Lesson 1 for more information about your home page.

Fortunately, there's a way to customize exactly what appears on your home page. You can choose which updates you want to view and which you want to hide, including content from your connections, groups, applications, and more.

To customize your home page settings:

1. Click the Account & Settings link on the top navigation menu.

2. On the Account & Settings page, click the Network Updates link in the Home Page Settings section. The Network Updates page opens, shown in Figure 4.3.

3. Specify how many updates you want to view on your home page. The default is 15, but you can choose from 10 to 25 updates.

4. Specify whether you want to Show or Hide each of the identified updates.

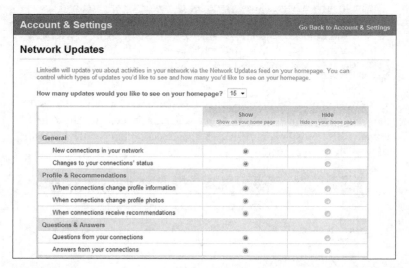

FIGURE 4.3   Customize the content that appears on your home page.

5. Click the Save Changes button. LinkedIn immediately makes the specified changes to your home page.

Subscribing to RSS Feeds

If you use a feed reader such as My Yahoo!, Google Reader, Newsgator, Bloglines, or Netvibes to subscribe to and read your favorite blog and news feeds, you might be interested in adding several LinkedIn feeds.

PLAIN ENGLISH: **RSS**

RSS stands for Really Simple Syndication, a popular format for web feeds. Content publishers can syndicate their content with a feed, making it available for users to subscribe to it and view with feed reader applications. Feeds for blog content are most common, but you can also create a feed for web content such as the content on LinkedIn. The advantage of feeds for the user is that you can view frequently updated content from your favorite blogs, podcasts, news sites, and other websites in one place. The standard feed icon is a small orange square with white radio waves, letting you know that the content is available via feed for your subscription.

To subscribe to LinkedIn feeds, click the Account & Settings link on the top navigation menu. On the Account & Settings page, click the Your Private RSS Feeds link in the RSS Settings section to open the LinkedIn RSS Feeds page, shown in Figure 4.4.

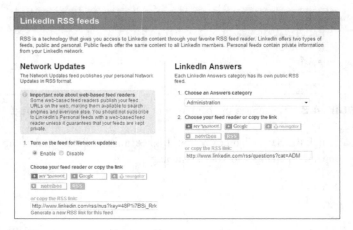

FIGURE 4.4   You can view LinkedIn content with your favorite feed reader.

PLAIN ENGLISH: **Private Feeds Versus Public Feeds**

It's important to understand the difference between a private feed and a public feed. LinkedIn private feeds contain personal data such as your updates and your connections' updates and are meant for your private viewing. Public feeds contain data available for public viewing on the web, such as the content in LinkedIn Answers.

LinkedIn offers a private feed of the network updates that appear on your home page.

CAUTION: **Ensuring Feed Privacy**

Be careful not to publish your private feed on the web. If you use a web-based feed reader, verify that your data will remain private if you don't want others to view your LinkedIn network updates.

To subscribe to this feed, select the Enable option button and choose your favorite feed reader from the buttons that appear. You can also copy the RSS link and use it in another feed reader if you prefer.

Subscribing to public feeds of your favorite LinkedIn Answers categories is another option. Each category maintains its own feed, so you can subscribe to one or more feeds based on your personal interests.

To do so, select a category from the drop-down list and click the button for your preferred feed reader. You can also copy the RSS link to use it in another feed reader.

TIP: **Subscribe to LinkedIn News**

LinkedIn also offers an RSS feed for LinkedIn news updates. To access this feed, go to http://learn.linkedin.com/whats-new/ and click the orange RSS feed icon to subscribe with your favorite feed reader.

Customizing Group Invitations Settings

By default, you will receive group invitations from your connections. If you don't want to receive these invitations, you can block them.

To do so, click the Account & Settings link on the top navigation menu. On the Account & Settings page, click the Group Invitation Filtering link in the Groups section to open the Group Invitation Settings page.

This page offers two choices for handling group invitations:

▶ I am open to receiving group invitations. This is the default option that LinkedIn recommends.

▶ I am not interested in receiving any group invitations. LinkedIn blocks all future group invitations, and you no longer receive them.

> TIP: **View Group Invitations Only on the Web**
>
> Rather than blocking all group invitations, you can specify to view them online rather than receiving them by email. See the section entitled "Customizing Email Notification Settings," earlier in this lesson for more information.

See Lesson 11, "Working with LinkedIn Groups," for more information on creating and using LinkedIn groups.

Customizing Your LinkedIn Personal Information

To customize your LinkedIn personal information, click the Account & Settings link on the top navigation menu.

The Personal Information section on the Account & Settings page provides links to modify the following data:

▶ **Name and Location**. Update your name and location. Additionally, specify the display name you want others to see. If you have strong privacy concerns, you can choose to display only your first name and last initial (such as Patrice R.) to people who aren't your connections. Displaying your full name will yield better results.

▶ **Email Address**. Add or delete email addresses and specify your primary email address where LinkedIn sends all messages.

TIP: **Add All Your Email Accounts to the Email Addresses Page**

Enter all the email addresses you use on the Email Addresses page. This includes your work email, personal email, and school email if you're a recent graduate or still use a university email account. When people invite you to connect, LinkedIn matches the email address they enter for you to your LinkedIn account. Entering all your email accounts helps ensure a match.

NOTE: **The Importance of Confirming Your Email Address**

Remember that many LinkedIn features aren't available until you confirm your email address. If you haven't done so yet, or didn't receive your original confirmation email, you can request another confirmation message on this page.

▶ **Change Password**. Specify a new password to use. Changing passwords on occasion is a good security measure. Also, remember to create a strong password that includes a combination of uppercase and lowercase letters, numbers, and symbols.

▶ **Close Your Account**. Close your account and specify your reason for doing so. Keep in mind that if you choose this option, you'll lose all your LinkedIn connections and will no longer have access to the site.

Customizing Your Privacy Settings

LinkedIn enables you to specify privacy settings for the data you display on the LinkedIn site and for the way LinkedIn uses your personal information.

> TIP: **Read LinkedIn's Privacy Policy**
>
> To learn more about LinkedIn's privacy policy, click the Privacy Policy link on LinkedIn's bottom navigation menu.

To customize your privacy settings, click the Account & Settings link on the top navigation menu. Next, click one of the following links in the Privacy Settings section of the Account & Settings page:

▶ **Research Surveys**. Specify whether you want to receive invitations to participate in LinkedIn online market research surveys.

▶ **Connections Browse**. By default, LinkedIn allows your direct connections to browse a list of your other connections. This can provide a useful way to develop your network, as it's quite likely that you may know some of your connections' connections. If you want to hide your connections list, however, you can choose to do so on the Connections Browse page. Your connections will still be able to view shared connections, however.

▶ **Profile Views**. The LinkedIn home page displays a box titled Who's Viewed My Profile that provides information about the people who visit your profile. You can customize what, if anything, LinkedIn publishes about you when you visit a LinkedIn member's profile. Options include displaying your name and headline, anonymous profile characteristics (such as industry and title), or nothing at all. If you're using LinkedIn as a business development tool, you might want others to know that you visited their profile. Otherwise, you might prefer complete or partial anonymity.

▶ **Viewing Profile Photos**. You can choose whose photos you want
to view. Options include all photos, no photos, or only photos of
people in your network or people who are your connections.

TIP: **Determine Who Can View Your Photo**

To specify who can view *your* photo, go to the Account & Settings
page and click the My Profile Photo link in the Profile Settings section.

▶ **Profile and Status Updates**. When you update your status,
modify your profile, or make recommendations, LinkedIn notifies your connections of these changes and publishes them in
company and industry updates. For most people, this provides
good exposure on the LinkedIn network. If you want to block
these notifications, however, you can do so. LinkedIn handles
profile update notifications and status update notifications sepa-
rately, so you can choose to participate in one, both, or neither.

▶ **Service Provider Directory**. LinkedIn publishes a service
provider directory for members who offer professional services.
If another member recommends you, you can choose whether
you want to be listed in the service provider directory. For most
people, this is a great form of free publicity. If you're a corporate employee, however, you may not want to be included if you
perform professional services only on occasion. See Lesson 14,
"Using LinkedIn Service Providers," for more information about
becoming a service provider.

▶ **Partner Advertising**. LinkedIn analyzes anonymous data from
your profile, such as your industry, to customize the advertise-
ments it displays and the content you view on partner sites (such
as nytimes.com). For example, if you specify Banking as your
industry, you'll view ads that are relevant to professionals in that
industry. If you don't want LinkedIn to use your personal data in
this way, you can opt out of this service.

▶ **Authorized Applications**. The Authorized Applications page
enables you to remove LinkedIn applications you installed. You

can also remove access to external websites that you previously allowed to access your LinkedIn data, such as Simply Hired or Business Exchange. See Lesson 13, "Using LinkedIn Applications," for more information about how to use LinkedIn applications.

Specifying How You Want to Use the LinkedIn Network

The final section of the Account & Settings page enables you to let LinkedIn know how you plan to use your LinkedIn network. For example, you can let LinkedIn know that you want to find a job, hire employees, sell products or services, and so forth. Click the Using Your Network link to provide LinkedIn with this informational data.

Summary

In this lesson, you learned how to customize your LinkedIn settings for optimal efficiency and privacy. This often one-time effort will pay off in the end with a much easier, more streamlined system for using LinkedIn.

Managing and Updating Your Profile

In this lesson, you'll learn how to update your LinkedIn status and profile, promote your profile on the web, create a profile in another language, and print and download your profile.

Understanding the Importance of a Current Profile

Keeping your profile current is critical to your success on LinkedIn. Creating your initial profile may be a one-time task, but you need to update it regularly to let others know you're an active participant on LinkedIn. In addition to updating your actual profile, LinkedIn enables you to post frequent status updates to inform your network about your activities and accomplishments.

Updating Your Status

LinkedIn status updates let you communicate important news to LinkedIn members in 140 characters or less. When you update your status, this text appears on your profile and on the Network Updates section of your connections' home page.

Brevity is the key to a status update: You need to express important information concisely. You can include links in status updates but no text formatting. If you're familiar with Twitter, you'll understand the concept of brief text updates. However, unlike Twitter, LinkedIn doesn't display a list of all your prior updates. Your status update remains on your profile indefinitely until you either delete it or replace it with a new status update.

Although status updates are a fun way to let your connections know what's new in your life, they are also a strategic networking tool. Keep your goals in mind and post updates that help achieve them. Here are some examples:

- ▶ Michelle Andrews is recruiting SAP business analysts.

- ▶ Anna Romanova just posted a new blog entry: 10 Tips for Healthcare Marketing http://bit.ly/15LcqU.

- ▶ Sam Wong is planning a career change to executive coaching.

- ▶ Patrice-Anne Rutledge just released her latest book, *Sams Teach Yourself LinkedIn in 10 Minutes*.

CAUTION: **Avoid Sales Pitches in Your Status Updates**
Although a well-crafted status update can be an effective marketing and publicity tool, avoid overt sales pitches in your status updates. A status update is a conversation with your network, not an advertisement.

TIP: **Use a URL Shortening Service to Include Links in Your Status Updates**
If the link you want to include in your status update exceeds the 140-character limit, you can use a URL shortening service. bit.ly (http://bit.ly) is one service that shortens URLs and tracks how many people click on your link.

The fastest way to update your status is in the Network Updates section on your home page (see Figure 5.1).

Enter your status update in this text box

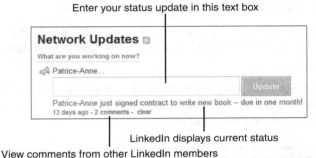

LinkedIn displays current status

View comments from other LinkedIn members

FIGURE 5.1 Use a status update to let other LinkedIn members know what you're doing.

Enter your status in the text box labeled What Are You Working on Now? and click the Update button.

Alternatively, you can use the status update pop-up box to update your status. You can access this box in two ways:

▶ Click the What Are You Working On? link in the profile summary box below the left navigation menu. If your status already appears, click the Edit link.

▶ Click the Edit My Profile link on the expanded left navigation menu. Then click the What Are You Working On? link at the top of your profile. Again, if you have a current status, this link is replaced with the Edit link.

Figure 5.2 illustrates the status update pop-up box.

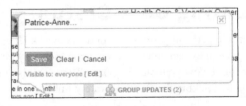

FIGURE 5.2 You can also enter a status update in this pop-up box.

Enter your status in the text box and click the Save button.

The Visible To field tells you who can view your status updates. If you want to change this, click the Edit link next to this field to open the Status Visibility page.

On this page, you can specify whether you want your status updates visible to your connections, to your network, or to everyone. Click the Save Settings button to save your changes.

TIP: **Use Status Updates to Gain Exposure Across the Entire LinkedIn Network**

Unless you have specific privacy concerns or communicate information pertinent only to your own connections, allowing everyone on LinkedIn to view your status updates provides the maximum exposure.

To delete a status update, click the Clear link below your status on your home page or in the status update pop-up box. Entering a new status update also removes your previous update.

TIP: **Update Multiple Social Networks at Once**

If you update your status on multiple social networking sites, consider using a free service such as Ping.fm (http://ping.fm). Ping.fm enables you to simultaneously post updates to sites such as LinkedIn, Facebook, and Twitter.

Commenting on a Status

When your status appears in your connections' Network Updates section on their home page, they can enter their own comments by clicking the Add Comment link below your status update. They can also send you a private message by clicking the Reply Privately link.

If your connections have entered comments about your status update, you'll see a link beneath your posted status update on your home page and on your profile. The link tells you how many comments you have (for example, 2 Comments). Click this link to view your comments and add your own feedback to the discussion.

TIP: **Add Comments to Participate in the LinkedIn Community**

Adding your own comments to your connections' status updates is a good way to stay in touch and maintain visibility.

Updating Your Profile

Even if you create a thorough profile when you first sign up for LinkedIn, you'll eventually want to update it with recent information.

You should update your LinkedIn profile whenever your employment status changes, you receive a degree or certification, win an award, learn a new skill, start a new business, achieve a career milestone, or change your LinkedIn goals. To update your profile, click the Edit My Profile link in the expanded left navigation menu. The Profile page opens with the Edit My Profile tab active, shown in Figure 5.3.

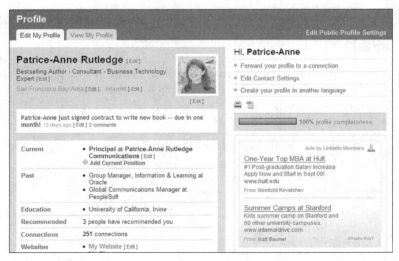

FIGURE 5.3   Be sure to update your profile regularly with new information.

The Edit My Profile tab is the same place you first created your profile, so you should already be familiar with its content. After you first enter profile data, links such as Add Past Position or Add Education disappear. Instead, click the Edit link next to any field you want to update. The appropriate LinkedIn page opens, where you can make any required changes.

You can also click the Current, Past, Education, Recommended, Connections, and Website links to enter data or make changes in those sections.

See Lesson 2, "Creating Your Profile," for more information about the content you can enter on the Edit My Profile tab.

CAUTION: **Don't Let Your Profile Get Outdated**

Although it's not necessary to update your profile every week, you shouldn't let it get outdated either. If it's obvious that you haven't touched your profile in months, or years, LinkedIn members might not bother contacting you for what could have been a lucrative opportunity for you.

Promoting Your Profile on the Web

With your permission, LinkedIn makes a public version of your profile available for view and search on the web. Figure 5.4 shows a sample LinkedIn profile link in Google search results.

TIP: **Promote Your LinkedIn Profile in Print**

Although promoting your profile online is most common, many LinkedIn members also print their LinkedIn profile URL on business cards, brochures, and other marketing materials.

Patrice-Anne Rutledge - LinkedIn
San Francisco Bay Area - Bestselling Author - Consultant - Business Technology Expert
View **Patrice-Anne Rutledge's** professional profile on **LinkedIn**. **LinkedIn** is the world's largest
business network, helping professionals like **Patrice-Anne ...**
www.**linkedin**.com/in/**patriceannerutledge** - 19k - Cached - Similar pages

FIGURE 5.4   Your LinkedIn public profile appears in Google search results.

To customize the appearance of your public profile, click the Account &
Settings link on the top navigation menu and click the Public Profile link
on the Account & Settings page.

Lesson 2, "Creating Your Profile," provided details on how to manage
your public profile. As a reminder, here are tips to maximize your profile's online visibility:

- ▶ Customize your public profile URL to make it user-friendly,
  such as http://www.linkedin.com/in/patriceannerutledge.

- ▶ Select the Full View option on the Public Profile page and place
  a check mark next to all fields you want to appear on your public profile.

- ▶ Preview your public profile to ensure that you like how it
  appears to others on the web.

In addition to maintaining a public profile, you can also post a LinkedIn
button on your website, blog, or online resume. Figure 5.5 shows a sample button.

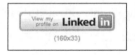

FIGURE 5.5   Site visitors can click your LinkedIn button to view your profile.

Click the Customized Buttons link on the Public Profile page to open the
Promote Your Profile! page, where you can select the button style you
prefer. LinkedIn offers a special button for TypePad users, but you can
place your button on any blog or website. For example, a blog sidebar is a
great place for a LinkedIn button. Copy the HTML code LinkedIn provides and paste it into your own site.

A third way to promote your LinkedIn profile on the web is to include a link to your public profile URL on the following:

- ▶ Your email signature

- ▶ Your online business card

- ▶ Other social sites, such as Technorati, Naymz, and Facebook

> TIP: **Promote Your LinkedIn Profile on Facebook**
> If you use Facebook (www.facebook.com), consider installing the My LinkedIn Profile application on your Facebook profile.

Creating a Profile in Another Language

English is the primary language on LinkedIn, but LinkedIn is a decidedly international network with more than half its members residing outside the United States. In Europe, for example, LinkedIn is the number one professional networking site in 43 countries. To meet the needs of its many international members, LinkedIn offers several foreign language features.

The LinkedIn interface is available in four languages: English, French, Spanish, and German. To view LinkedIn in another language, click the Language link on the top navigation menu and select your preferred language. Figure 5.6 shows the LinkedIn interface in French.

FIGURE 5.6   The LinkedIn interface is available in French as well as three other languages.

Keep in mind that even if you view the LinkedIn interface in another language, this doesn't translate the user-generated content of an individual member's profile. The profile content remains in the original language the member used to create it.

To display your profile content in another language, you need to create a profile in that language. For example, someone involved in international business or residing in a country with more than one official language might want to create profiles in multiple languages.

To create a profile in another language, follow these steps:

1. Click the Edit My Profile link on the expanded left navigation menu.

2. Click the Create Your Profile in Another Language link, which appears at the top of the right column of the Edit My Profile tab. The Create Your Profile in Another Language page opens.

3. Select the language for your profile from the Language drop-down list. LinkedIn currently supports more than 40 languages. To create a profile in a language that LinkedIn doesn't support, select Other.

4. Enter your First Name, Last Name, and a Former/Maiden Name, if applicable.

5. Enter your Professional Headline.

6. Click the Create Profile button to return to the Edit My Profile page.

7. Enter your profile content in your target language, just as you did for your English-language profile.

LinkedIn members can choose to view your profile in another language by selecting their preferred language from the Profile drop-down list in the upper-right corner of your profile, shown in Figure 5.7.

FIGURE 5.7   Members can choose to view your profile content in any of the language versions you create.

NOTE: **What If the Profile Drop-Down List Is Missing?**
Only those languages for which you create a profile are available in the drop-down list. If you have a profile only in English, the Profile field won't be visible.

Printing and Downloading Your Profile

You can print and download your profile, or the profile of another LinkedIn member, by clicking one of the icons in the upper-right corner of a profile, shown in Figure 5.8.

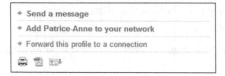

FIGURE 5.8   Print or download your profile.

Your options include

- ▶ **Print This Profile**. Opens the Print dialog box in which you can specify print options and print a profile.

- ▶ **Download as PDF**. Creates a PDF document from your profile that you can view with Adobe Reader (get.adobe.com/reader).

- ▶ **Download vCard**. Downloads your profile in the vCard format, which is a file format used for electronic business cards. This option appears only for your own profile or for your connections.

Summary

In this lesson, you learned how to update your status and profile, promote your profile on the web, create a profile in another language, and print and download your profile. Next, learn the many ways to communicate with other members and become part of the LinkedIn community.

LESSON 6

Communicating with Other LinkedIn Members

In this lesson, you'll learn about the LinkedIn network and the many ways to communicate with other LinkedIn members.

Understanding Your LinkedIn Network

Before you start communicating with others on LinkedIn, you need to understand how LinkedIn classifies its members in terms of their connections to you. This distinction is important because it determines what, if any, restrictions LinkedIn places on your ability to contact people.

Your LinkedIn network consists of three levels of connections:

▶ **1st degree connections**. LinkedIn members you connect with directly. Either you sent them an invitation to connect and they accepted, or you accepted their invitation. Your connection list on your profile displays your 1st degree connections. When LinkedIn refers to "your connections," this means your 1st degree connections.

▶ **2nd degree connections**. LinkedIn members who connect directly with your 1st degree connections.

▶ **3rd degree connections**. LinkedIn members who connect directly with your 2nd degree connections.

For example, if you connect directly with your colleague Nicole, she is your 1st degree connection. If Nicole connects directly to Ben, her former classmate, Ben is your 2nd degree connection. If Ben connects directly with Drake, one of his co-workers, Drake is your 3rd degree connection.

LinkedIn also considers fellow members of groups as part of your network. See Lesson 11, "Working with LinkedIn Groups," for more information about LinkedIn groups.

PLAIN ENGLISH: **My Network**

Your LinkedIn network (termed "My Network") differs from the entire LinkedIn network, which consists of all LinkedIn members. At the time of this printing, the entire LinkedIn network includes more than 40 million members.

TIP: **View Your Network Statistics**

To view how many people are in each level of your network, click the Network Statistics link in the expanded left navigation menu.

Understanding InMail, Introductions, and LinkedIn Messages

LinkedIn offers several ways to communicate with other members. The type of communication you can send depends on how you're connected to these members. Your choices include

▶ **Messages**. Messages are the primary form of communication on LinkedIn. You can send messages to your direct connections as well as to the people who belong to the same LinkedIn groups as you do. If you can send a message to someone, the Send Message link appears next to their name on their profile and in search results. See "Sending Messages" later in this lesson for more information. Although you'll often see the term "message" used generically to refer to all items in your Inbox, it is a specific type of communication in itself.

▶ **Invitations.** An invitation is a request to connect with another LinkedIn member. See Lesson 3, "Adding and Managing Connections," for more information about sending invitations.

▶ **InMail.** An InMail is a private message to or from a LinkedIn member who is not your connection. You can receive InMail free if you indicate that you are open to receiving InMail messages on the Account & Settings page. In general, sending InMail is a paid LinkedIn feature unless the recipient is a premium member who belongs to the OpenLink Network. See "Sending InMail" later in this lesson for more information.

▶ **Introductions.** An introduction provides a way to reach out to the people who are connected to your connections. By requesting an introduction through someone you already know, that person can introduce you to the person you're trying to reach. You can contact your 1st degree connections to request introductions to members who are 2nd and 3rd degree connections. Members with free accounts can have up to five introductions open at a time. See "Requesting Introductions" later in this lesson for more information.

Understanding Your Contact Options

Before you start communicating with another LinkedIn member, you need to understand your available options for contacting that particular person. When you view member profiles or their summary information from another part of the site, the icons next to a member's name tell you how you're connected (see Figure 6.1).

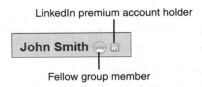

FIGURE 6.1   The icons next to a member's name tell you how you're connected.

These icons identify 1st, 2nd, and 3rd degree connections; fellow group members; and LinkedIn premium account holders.

> NOTE: **Some LinkedIn Members Have No Icons**
>
> Members who display no icons next to their names are out of your network, don't share any groups, and aren't premium account holders.

The links that display to the right of a member's name let you know what contact options are available. These include

- **Send Message**. Send a message to a direct connection or group member.

- **Send InMail**. Send an InMail to someone who isn't in your network. This option doesn't appear for members to whom you can send a message because it wouldn't make sense to pay to contact someone you can communicate with freely. If you click the Send InMail link and don't have a premium account, LinkedIn prompts you to sign up for one before you can proceed.

- **Send InMail (Free)**. Send an OpenLink message to a member of the OpenLink Network. LinkedIn members who hold premium accounts can offer you the option of sending them free InMail. See Lesson 1, "Introducing LinkedIn," for more information about the OpenLink Network.

- **Get Introduced Through a Connection**. Request an introduction to this member through a 1st degree connection.

▶ **Add [person's first name] to Network**. Send an invitation to connect. See Lesson 3, "Adding and Managing Connections," for more information about sending connection requests.

▶ **Forward This Profile to a Connection**. Forward a member's profile to a member you know, as a way of informal introduction.

These are the link names that appear on an actual profile. The link names in search results are sometimes abbreviated.

CAUTION: **Not All Options Are Available for All Members**

Remember that you'll never see all of these options for any one member. For example, it wouldn't make sense to send InMail, request an introduction, or add to your network a member who is already your connection, so these options don't appear for your connections.

Managing Your Inbox

Your Inbox is the focal point for all your direct communication on LinkedIn. A summary of your five most recent Inbox items appears at the top of your home page. You can also click the Inbox link on the left navigation menu to open the Inbox page, shown in Figure 6.2.

The default view of your Inbox is the Received tab, which displays all the items you've received. If you have a lot of Inbox items and want to filter what you see, click the down arrow next to the Received heading and choose one of the available options. For example, you can choose to display only action items, messages, InMails, introductions, invitations, jobs, recommendations, or group messages.

Click to filter messages

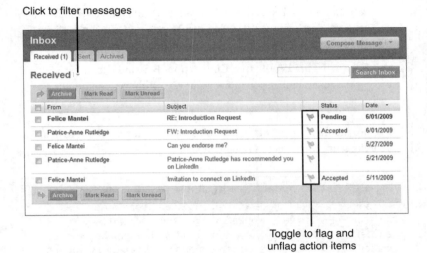

Toggle to flag and
unflag action items

FIGURE 6.2   Your Inbox is the focal point for your personal communications on LinkedIn.

> TIP: **Search for Specific Content**
>
> In addition to filtering Inbox items, you can also search for a specific message. Enter a keyword in the text box on the right side of the page and click the Search Inbox button. LinkedIn displays all messages containing that search term. For example, you could search for a person's name or a word or phrase in the subject line or message text.

From the Received tab, you can

- ▶ Sort your messages. Click one of the message headings (From, Subject, Status, or Date) to sort based on that heading.

- ▶ Archive a message. Select the check box to the left of the message you want to move to the Archive folder and click the Archive button. It's a good idea to archive old or resolved messages to keep your Inbox focused on your current action items.

> **CAUTION: You Can't Delete Messages from Your Inbox**
> LinkedIn doesn't let you delete messages from your Inbox. If you want to remove messages, simply archive the messages you no longer need to view.

▶ Mark a message as read or unread. By default, new messages appear in bold text to signify they have not yet been read. After you read a message, the message no longer is boldfaced in your Inbox. To change this, select the check box to the left of a message and click either the Mark Read or Mark Unread button.

▶ Flag a message as an action item for follow-up. By default, new messages include a flag icon to the right of the subject line, flagging it as an action item. Click the flag icon, which serves as a toggle, to flag or unflag a message for action.

The Inbox also includes two other tabs. The Sent tab displays all your sent messages and the Archived tab displays all the messages you archived.

Each message also lists a status. When a new message arrives, its status displays as Pending. Based on the action you take on each message, your status changes. Status options include

▶ **Accepted**. You accepted the message, such as an invitation to connect.

▶ **Bounced**. The message bounced when sent to an email provider.

▶ **Don't Know/Doesn't Know**. The message, such as an invitation to connect, was rejected when the recipient clicked the I Don't Know This User button. LinkedIn lists the status as "Don't Know" if you clicked the button. The status is "Doesn't Know" if you sent the request that was rejected.

▶ **In Progress**. Identifies an InMail or introduction request that is still an action item for one of the people involved.

▶ **Replaced**. Another message has replaced this message and you can no longer respond to it. For example, someone sent you a recommendation request and then resent it when you didn't respond.

▶ **Replied**. You replied to the message.

▶ **Sent**. You sent this message. If the message was a request, the recipient hasn't accepted it yet.

▶ **Withdrawn**. The sender has withdrawn this message, request, or invitation.

You can also send messages directly from the Inbox. Click the Compose Message button to open the Compose Your Message page and send a message to a connection. For other options, click the down arrow to the right of the Compose Message button. From the drop-down list, you can choose to

▶ Send a message to a connection (same result as clicking the Compose Message button)

▶ Send InMail or an introduction

▶ Send invitation

▶ Send recommendation

▶ Request recommendation

▶ Send job notification

Refer to other sections in this lesson and other lessons in this book for more information about each specific type of communication.

Sending Messages

To send a message to a 1st degree connection or group member, follow these steps:

1. Click the Compose Message link on the expanded left navigation menu to open the Compose Your Message page, shown in Figure 6.3.

Start typing a name to find a match

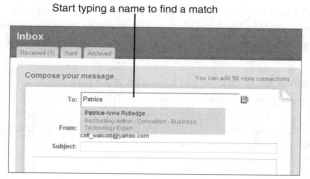

FIGURE 6.3 Sending a direct message to one your LinkedIn connections.

2. In the To field, start typing the name of your connection and wait for LinkedIn to find a match.

TIP: **Send a Message to Multiple Connections**
Alternatively, click the address book icon to open your connection list. With the address book, you can search for the person you want to reach or select multiple recipients for your message. LinkedIn allows you to send a message to up to 50 connections at one time.

3. Enter a Subject for your message.

4. Enter your message in the text box.

5. If you're sending a message to multiple recipients and don't want to disclose this information, remove the check mark before the Allow Recipients to See Each Other's Names and Email Addresses check box (selected by default).

6. To email yourself a copy of your message, select the Send Me a Copy check box. Your message already appears in your Sent folder by default.

7. Click the Send button. LinkedIn sends your message to the recipient and notifies you that your message was sent.

Although clicking the Compose Message link is the primary way to send messages on LinkedIn, you can also send messages by clicking the Send Message link in a profile, on your home page, or in search results.

TIP: **Other Ways to Contact LinkedIn Members**
The profiles of your direct connections also display their external email address in the Your Private Info About [First Name] box. Some members include their email addresses directly on their profiles for the entire LinkedIn network to see.

Reading and Replying to Messages

You can open your messages from the Inbox preview on your home page or from the Inbox itself. (Access it by clicking the Inbox link on the left navigation menu.)

Click the Subject line link of any message to open it. Figure 6.4 illustrates a sample message.

FIGURE 6.4   View a message and reply to it.

The buttons that appear at the bottom of a message vary depending upon the message type and what actions you can take. For example, a basic message includes the Reply button, a recommendation request includes the Write a Recommendation button, and an invitation to connect includes the Accept button and I Don't Know This User button.

Sending InMail

As you learned earlier in this chapter, InMail enables you to contact LinkedIn members who aren't in your network. In an effort to manage spam, LinkedIn requires members to pay to send InMail. InMail is most useful for members who want to contact a wide variety of people, such as recruiters or individuals using LinkedIn for business development.

LinkedIn premium accounts enable you to send a fixed number of InMail messages per month. To learn more about LinkedIn premium accounts and InMail, click the Upgrade Your Account link on the bottom navigation menu. You can also purchase individual InMails at $10 each. To do so, click the Account & Settings link on the top navigation menu and then click the Purchase link in the Account section. This is cost-efficient only if you want to contact just a few people by InMail.

TIP: **When You Can Send Free InMail**

If you see the word "Free" immediately following a Send InMail link, you can send InMail to this LinkedIn member at no charge. To enable members to send you free InMail, you must participate in the OpenLink Network, a premium feature.

See Lesson 1 to learn more about the OpenLink Network and premium account options.

To determine the InMail options available for a particular member, view the contact options on that person's profile (see Figure 6.5).

FIGURE 6.5   Determine the InMail options for a particular LinkedIn member.

NOTE: **Where Is the Send InMail Link?**

You won't see any Send InMail link for members who indicate on the Account & Settings page that they aren't open to receiving InMail. InMail isn't an option for your connections, either. You can contact them directly at no cost to either party.

To send InMail to a LinkedIn member, follow these steps:

1. Click the Send InMail link on the profile of the person you want to reach. If you're sending paid InMail, the Compose Your Message page opens. If you're sending free InMail, the Compose Your OpenLink Message page opens (see Figure 6.6). These pages contain identical information.

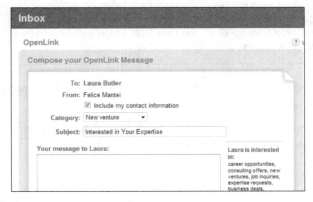

FIGURE 6.6   Sending free InMail to members of the OpenLink Network.

2. If you don't want to share your contact information with the person you want to reach, remove the check mark from the Include My Contact Information check box (selected by default). In general, it's a good idea to share contact information.

3. In the Category drop-down list, select the reason for your InMail. Options include career opportunity, consulting offer, new venture, job inquiry, expertise request, business deal, reference request, or get back in touch.

4. In the Subject field, enter the subject of your InMail.

5. In the text box, enter your message. To increase your chances of a positive reply, be as specific as possible.

6. Click the Send button to send your InMail. If the recipient doesn't respond to the InMail within seven days, the message expires.

For more information about InMail, see "Understanding InMail, Introductions, and LinkedIn Messages" in this lesson and see Lesson 1.

TIP: **Consider Alternatives to InMail**

Although InMail is an effective LinkedIn communication tool, it comes at a price. If you want to contact someone you don't know and don't want to pay to send InMail, you have several other options. You could join a group that this person belongs to and then send a message or invitation to connect as a fellow group member. You could also request an introduction through a mutual connection. Alternatively, you could choose to contact the individual outside LinkedIn by accessing the website links and external email information individuals provide on their profiles.

Requesting Introductions

Requesting an introduction is a good way to connect with people in your network whom you don't connect with directly. Although you can send an invitation to connect to someone you don't know, you might want to consider requesting an introduction through a shared connection for important communications. An introduction can carry more weight than a cold contact.

For example, let's say that you're connected to your former manager Felice (1st degree connection) and Felice is connected to Dalton (2nd degree connection), a manager at another local company. You're very interested in working in Dalton's department, but you don't know him and haven't seen any posted job openings. Rather than sending Dalton an email and resume as a "cold contact," you could send an introduction request through Felice.

Often you'll know already how you're connected to the person you want to reach, but you can also determine this by viewing the How You're Connected To [First Name] on your target contact's profile. If you don't already know of a common connection, this box could list a name you recognize.

Here are several tips for making the most of LinkedIn introductions:

▶ Talk to your 1st degree connection before sending an introduction request on LinkedIn. Your connection might have information that's pertinent to your request. For example, if you're trying to reach someone about job opportunities, your connection might know if your target is hiring or if there's a more suitable person to contact.

▶ Focus on introductions to 2nd degree connections for best results. Although you can request an introduction to a 3rd degree connection, this requires two intermediaries. In many cases, the second intermediary (your 2nd degree connection passing on your request to your 3rd degree connection) might not even know you.

▶ Make your introduction request concise and specific. A vague request to "get to know" someone isn't nearly as effective as stating your specific purpose, such as seeking employment, recruiting for a job, offering consulting services, and so forth.

▶ Keep in mind that you can have only five open introductions at one time with a free LinkedIn personal account. Find out how many introductions you still have available by clicking the Account & Settings link in the top navigation menu and viewing your account summary. To increase your number of open introductions, you need to upgrade to a premium account. LinkedIn recommends using introductions judiciously rather than as a tool to contact hundreds of members.

To request an introduction, follow these steps:

1. Click the Get Introduced Through a Connection link on the profile of the person you want to reach. The Introductions page opens, shown in Figure 6.7.

FIGURE 6.7 Requesting an introduction to someone your connection knows.

TIP: **Other Ways to Request an Introduction**
You can also request an introduction by clicking the Get Introduced link in search results or group member lists.

2. If you don't want to share your contact information with the person you want to reach, remove the check mark from the Include My Contact Information check box (selected by default). In general, it's a good idea to share contact information.

3. From the Category drop-down list, select the reason for your introduction request. Options include career opportunity, consulting offer, new venture, job inquiry, expertise request, business deal, reference request, or get back in touch.

4. In the Subject field, enter the subject of your request.

5. In the first text box, enter your message to the person you want to be introduced to.

6. In the second text box, enter a brief note to the person you want to make the referral (your 1st degree connection).

7. Click the Send button to send your introduction request.

Your 1st degree connection receives your request and can choose to forward it to your target connection with comments or decline your request. If your request wasn't clear, your connection might ask you for more information.

See the following section, "Managing Introduction Requests," for more information about the next step in the process.

Managing Introduction Requests

In addition to requesting your own introductions to others, you might also receive introduction requests. For example, LinkedIn members might ask you to facilitate an introduction to one of your connections or might ask your connection to facilitate an introduction to you.

To review and respond to introduction requests, follow these steps:

1. Click the Inbox link on the left navigation menu to open your Inbox.

2. If you have many messages in your Inbox, select Introductions from the Received drop-down list. Your Inbox displays only your introduction requests. Alternatively, you can also view new introduction requests in your Inbox preview on your home page or receive them by email. (Specify this on the Account & Settings page.)

3. To open the request, click the subject line link. Figure 6.8 illustrates a sample introduction request.

FIGURE 6.8 Forward an introduction request on to one of your connections.

4. Click the Forward Introduction button to forward the request to your connection.

> NOTE: **Declining or Archiving an Introduction Request**
>
> If you don't want to make the introduction, click the Decline Introduction button. Alternatively, click the Archive button to move the request to your Archive folder where you can take action on the request later. Introduction requests remain active for six months.

5. Enter any additional comments in the text box and click the Forward Message button.

The target recipient receives your forwarded introduction request and can accept, decline, or archive it. Accepting the introduction enables the requestor and target to communicate with each other, but they still need to send an invitation request to become connections.

Summary

In this lesson, you learned about the many ways to communicate with other LinkedIn members and the options available based on their connection to you. Next, you'll learn how to search for people on LinkedIn.

LESSON 7

Searching on LinkedIn

In this lesson, you'll learn about LinkedIn quick searches, searching for people, and advanced search techniques.

Performing a Quick Search

LinkedIn is a large, complex network of information. You can greatly improve your chances of achieving your networking goals by learning how to find exactly what you want among 40 million member profiles and many more millions of answers, job postings, and group discussions. The easiest way to search for information on LinkedIn is to use the search box on LinkedIn's top navigation menu, shown in Figure 7.1.

FIGURE 7.1   Quickly search for information from anywhere on LinkedIn.

To perform a quick search, follow these steps:

1. Select the focus of your search from the drop-down list. Options include

   ► Search People (the default)

   ► Search Jobs

   ► Search Companies

   ► Search Answers

   ► Search Inbox

   ► Search Groups

2. Enter your search term in the text box. This might be a person's name, company name, job title, job skill, or a keyword, for example.

3. Click the Search button. LinkedIn displays search results. The format of the search results depends on the type of search you perform.

This lesson focuses on LinkedIn's most popular search type (the people search) and advanced search techniques. To learn more about searching for jobs, companies, answers, your inbox, and groups, refer to the lessons in this book that cover those topics.

Searching for People

The fastest way to search for people is to perform a quick search from the search box on LinkedIn's top navigation menu. For example, let's say that you're searching for your former colleague Felice Mantei. Enter her name in the search box and click the Search button. Your search results appear, shown in Figure 7.2.

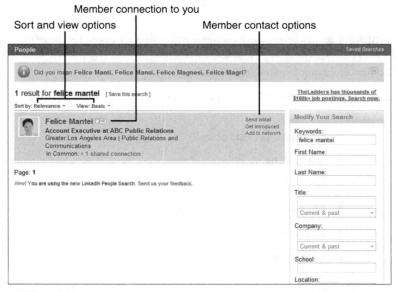

FIGURE 7.2 It's easy to find colleagues and classmates on LinkedIn.

NOTE: **LinkedIn Helps You Find Matches as You Type**
As you type, LinkedIn displays a drop-down list of potential matches in your network of connections. If you see a match in this list, click the member's name to open that member's profile.

Each LinkedIn member who matches your search results appears in a preview box that includes a photo, name, headline, location, industry, and information about shared connections and groups. Depending on the preview you're viewing, not all items might appear. For example, a member might choose not to upload a photo.

Icons appear to the right of each member's name indicating their connection to you, such as a 1st degree connection, 2nd degree connection, 3rd degree connection, or group member. For members who are out of your network, you may view the Out of Network designation next to their name or their name may be hidden from view.

See Lesson 6, "Communicating with Other LinkedIn Members," for a reminder of how LinkedIn classifies its members.

Hover over the preview of a specific LinkedIn member to view the available contact links (the preview box turns blue). Possible links include Send Message, Get Introduced, Send InMail, or Add to Network. The options available depend on your connection to the particular member. For example, it wouldn't make sense for you to send InMail or get introduced to someone you already connect with. See Lesson 6, "Communicating with Other LinkedIn Members," for more information about the available options for contacting others on LinkedIn.

NOTE: **LinkedIn Limits the Number of Members You Can View**
With a personal account, you can view 100 results at a time. To view more results, you need to upgrade to a premium account. To learn more about premium accounts, click the Upgrade Your Account link on the bottom navigation menu.

Narrowing People Search Results

When you search for the name of a specific individual, the search results should display a short list (unless the individual has a very common name). But what if you can't remember someone's last name or you're searching for LinkedIn members who meet specific criteria such CPAs in the Indianapolis area? In this case, your search might return thousands of results, exceeding the 100-result viewing limits associated with a personal account.

There are two ways to handle this. One is to narrow the results that display on your search results page. The other is to perform an advanced search that targets very specific criteria.

On the search results page, you can sort the search results using the following criteria:

▶ **Relevance**. Displays search results in the order LinkedIn determines most appropriate based on keywords you enter and your network.

▶ **Relationship**. Displays search results based on their position in your network, in the following order: 1st degree connections, 2nd degree connections, fellow group members, and 3rd degree connections that are combined with out-of-network connections.

▶ **Relationship + Recommendation**. Displays search results by relationship. Those that have the most recommendations are listed first for each relationship category.

▶ **Keyword**. Displays search results that match your keywords without considering their placement in your network.

You can also customize the member information you preview in your search results. The options are

▶ **Basic**. Displays a photo, name, professional headline, location, industry, and details about shared connections.

▶ **Expanded**. Displays all the information from the basic view and current and past employment details.

▶ **Create a New View**. Opens the Create a New View pop-up box (see Figure 7.3) in which you can specify the exact information you want to display in the preview. Options include the data you can see in Basic and Expanded views and Recommendations, Groups, and number of Connections. Click the Save button to save your customized view for future use. Customized views are a premium feature for customers who upgrade to a paid account.

Create a new view   ⊠

Create a customized view of your search results. Choose the fields below. Please note, this is a premium feature offered free for a limited time.

☑ Headline   ☑ Current   ☑ Location
☑ Industry   ☑ Actions   ☑ In Common
☑ Past   ☑ Photo   ☑ Connections
☑ Recommendations   ☑ Groups

Name this view: My customized view

[Save] or Cancel

FIGURE 7.3   Customize exactly what you see in search results.

You can narrow your search results in the Modify Your Search box on the right side of your screen, shown in Figure 7.4.

In this box, you can narrow your search results by specifying any of the following criteria:

▶ **Keywords**. Enter a keyword that LinkedIn searches for in member profiles. The best keywords are terms that don't fit any of the other search criteria and are specific words that a member might include on a profile. For example, entering a name or location wouldn't be appropriate here, but terms such as Java, PMP, auditing, CPA, and so forth would work well.

▶ **First Name**. Enter the first name of the member you want to find.

FIGURE 7.4   Modify your search criteria to narrow your results.

▶ **Last Name**. Enter the last name of the member you want to find.

▶ **Title**. Enter a job title and specify in the drop-down list whether you want to search only for members who hold this title currently, in the past, or both currently and in the past.

▶ **Company**. Enter a company name and specify in the drop-down list whether you want to search only for members who work at this company currently, in the past, or both currently and in the past.

▶ **School**. Enter the name of a college or university.

▶ **Location**. Select a Country, Postal Code, and distance range.

▶ **My Network Only**. Select this check box if you want to search only within your network.

Click the Search button to update the search results.

To view even more search options, click the Show More link, which provides you with these additional options:

- **Industry**. Select the industries you want to include in your search.

- **Groups**. Select the groups you want to include in your search. Your choices include only those groups you currently belong to. If you don't belong to any groups, you won't see this option.

- **Language**. Select the languages in which you want to view profiles.

- **Interested In**. Select one of the following options: all users, potential employees, consultants/contractors, entrepreneurs, hiring managers, industry experts, or deal-making contacts. LinkedIn displays members who are potential matches based on their profile content.

- **Joined**. Select one of the following options: at any time, since your last login, in the last day, in the last week, in the last two weeks, in the last month, or in the last three months. Recruiters, for example, might use this option to receive notifications of new members who match the recruiters' job search criteria.

Again, click the Search button to update results.

Performing an Advanced People Search

If you want to search for very specific criteria, you can perform an advanced people search. An advanced search offers you the same options as the extended version of the Modify Your Search box on the search results page, but you can perform it all in one step. For example, you might enter a search term in the quick search box and then decide to narrow your results. But if you already know that you want to search for specific keywords, companies, or locations, for example, an advanced search is a more streamlined option.

To perform an advanced people search, select the Search People option (if it's not already selected by default) on the search box that appears on the top navigation menu and click the Advanced link. Figure 7.5 shows the Advanced Search page.

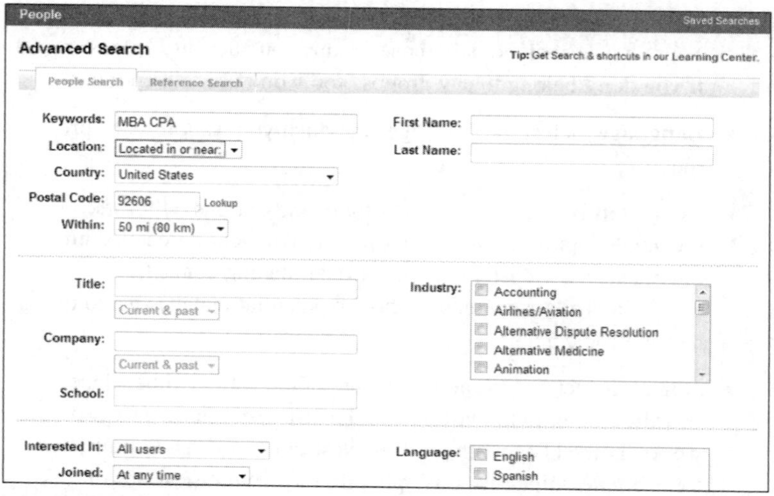

FIGURE 7.5   LinkedIn's advanced search options provide maximum flexibility in finding members who meet specific criteria.

Enter your search criteria on this page and click the Search button to display your search results. Refer to "Narrowing People Search Results," earlier in this lesson for descriptions of each field on this page.

> NOTE: **Performing a Reference Search**
>
> The Advanced Search page also includes a Reference Search tab in which you can search for potential references for a job candidate. See Web Lesson 1, "Recruiting Job Candidates," for more information about reference searches.

Saving a People Search

If you perform the same searches frequently, saving them can reduce
redundant data entry. To save a search for future use, follow these steps:

1. Click the Save This Search link on the search results page.

2. In the Save This Search pop-up box, enter a Search Name for
this search (see Figure 7.6).

Save this search   ⊠

You can save up to 3 searches to easily access from the results page. You can even
have LinkedIn run your search and email you the new results.

Search Name: CPA MBA 50 mi (80 km) 94566 |

Send by Email: Weekly   ▼

Save   or Cancel

Tip: Upgrade your account to save more than **3 searches**.

FIGURE 7.6   Saving a search saves you time.

3. In the Send by Email field, choose to receive email updates of
your search results: Weekly, Monthly, or Never. You don't have
to receive updates by email, but this can be a timesaver if you're
very interested in following updates to your saved search. For
example, recruiters might want to know about new LinkedIn
members who match specific search criteria. Or job seekers
might want to know about new LinkedIn members who work at
companies they're interested in working for.

NOTE: **LinkedIn Limits the Number of Searches You Can Save**

As a free personal account holder, you can save up to three searches and receive email updates either weekly or monthly. To save more
searches, click the Upgrade Your Account link to sign up for a premium account. If you want to receive daily email updates on your
saved searches, you must select the Pro account option.

4. Click the Save button to save your search.

To edit or delete your saved searches, click the Save Searches link in the upper-right corner of the search results page.

Using Advanced Search Techniques

LinkedIn offers several techniques for narrowing your search results even further. You can use these techniques when performing a quick search or when using the Advanced Search page. For example, you can search for phrases in quotation marks, use search operators such as NOT and OR, or enter complex criteria with a parenthetical search.

LinkedIn enables you to use specific search operators to define advanced criteria directly in the quick search box. For example, ccompany is the operator for current company and title is the operator for job title. Entering ccompany:Google title:director would quickly list all current Google employees with the title of director.

For more information about advanced search techniques, visit the LinkedIn Learning Center at http://learn.linkedin.com/linkedin-search. Scroll down the page to the "Advanced Search Tips" section.

Summary

In this lesson, you learned how to find information quickly and easily through LinkedIn's advanced search capabilities. Next, you'll learn about several tools that also enhance searching and other aspects of your LinkedIn experience.

Using LinkedIn Tools

In this lesson, you'll learn about the tools that enable you to access LinkedIn data from other websites and software.

Understanding LinkedIn Tools

LinkedIn offers several tools, toolbars, and widgets that enhance your LinkedIn experience, both on and off the site. Options include

- ▶ **Browser Toolbar**. Search and access LinkedIn data from Firefox or Internet Explorer.

- ▶ **JobsInsider**. Discover members of your LinkedIn network who work at companies whose job postings you're viewing. JobsInsider is included with the Browser Toolbar.

- ▶ **Outlook Toolbar**. Manage your LinkedIn network from Microsoft Outlook.

- ▶ **Email Signature**. Create a customized email signature from your profile data to use with popular email systems.

- ▶ **Google Toolbar Assistant**. Add a LinkedIn search button to the Google Toolbar.

- ▶ **Mac Search Widget**. Search LinkedIn from your Mac Dashboard.

- ▶ **Developer Widgets**. Use and develop widgets that integrate LinkedIn data with other websites.

- ▶ **Polls**. Poll LinkedIn members about pertinent business and professional topics. Polls are both a tool and an application. See Lesson 13, "Using LinkedIn Applications," for more information.

You can access LinkedIn tools from the Tools row on the bottom navigation menu.

Installing and Using the LinkedIn Firefox Browser Toolbar

The LinkedIn Firefox Browser Toolbar, also called the LinkedIn Companion for Firefox, is available for a PC or Mac running Firefox versions 2.0 or 3.0. System requirements include Windows XP/Vista or Mac OS X 10.2 or later.

TIP: **Mac Users Should Also Consider the Mac Search Widget**
Another option for Mac users is the Mac Search Widget, which enables you to search LinkedIn from your Mac Dashboard. The widget requires OS 10.4. To download the widget, click the Overview link on LinkedIn's bottom navigation menu and then click the Download It Now button in the Mac Search Widget section.

To install the LinkedIn Firefox Browser Toolbar, follow these steps:

1. Click the Browser Toolbar link on the bottom navigation menu. The LinkedIn Browser Toolbar page opens.

2. Click the Download It Now button below the Firefox Toolbar 3.1 heading.

3. Click the OK button to confirm that you are located in one of the countries listed in the pop-up box. Firefox might try to prevent you from installing the toolbar. If you receive a warning message, click the Allow button to continue installation.

4. Click the Install Now button in the window that appears.

5. Restart Firefox to complete your changes.

The toolbar now appears in Firefox (see Figure 8.1).

If the LinkedIn button doesn't appear on your browser toolbar, try one of the following:

▶ Verify that you meet all the listed system requirements.

▶ Click the View menu, click Toolbars, and then click Bookmarks Toolbar to display the Bookmarks toolbar on Firefox.

▶ Click the View menu, click Toolbars, and then click Customize. In the Customize Toolbars dialog box, select Icons and Text from the Show drop-down list, drag the LinkedIn icon to the toolbar, and click the Done button.

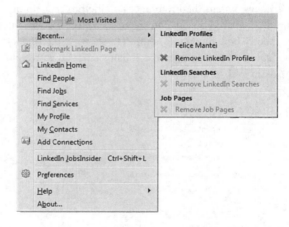

FIGURE 8.1 Use the LinkedIn Firefox Browser toolbar to locate information on LinkedIn.

Click the LinkedIn button on your browser toolbar to display a drop-down list of options. These include

- ▶ **Recent**. Displays links to your recent profile, recent searches, and job page views. To clear this data, click the Remove options.

- ▶ **Bookmark LinkedIn Page**. Lets you create a Firefox bookmark for an active LinkedIn page. This option is available only if you're viewing a LinkedIn page that you can bookmark, such as a profile, search results, or a job listing.

- ▶ **LinkedIn Home**. Takes you to LinkedIn's home page. This section also includes direct links to Find People, Find Jobs, Find Services, My Profile, My Contacts, and Add Connections.

- ▶ **LinkedIn JobsInsider**. Opens the LinkedIn JobsInsider window. See the "Using the JobsInsider" section later in this lesson for more information.

- ▶ **Preferences**. Opens the Preferences dialog box, shown in Figure 8.2, where you can enter your LinkedIn account information, specify how much information to show on the Recent menu, specify when to open the JobsInsider, and activate the InfoBox in Web email option.

FIGURE 8.2   Specify what you want to display on the Recent menu of the toolbar.

▶ **Help**. Opens a help file in which you can search for more information.

▶ **About**. Displays information about the toolbar.

To uninstall the toolbar, select Tools, Add-Ons from the Firefox menu and click the Uninstall button in the LinkedIn Companion for Firefox section.

Installing and Using the LinkedIn Internet Explorer Toolbar

The LinkedIn Internet Explorer Toolbar is available for the PC only, running Microsoft Windows 2000/XP, with Microsoft Internet Explorer 6.0 and 7.0.

To install the LinkedIn Internet Explorer Toolbar, follow these steps:

1. Click the Browser Toolbar link on the bottom navigation menu. The LinkedIn Browser Toolbar page opens.

2. Click the Download It Now button below the IE Toolbar 3.0 heading.

3. Click the OK button to confirm that you are located in one of the countries listed in the pop-up box.

4. Click the Run button. The LinkedIn Internet Explorer Toolbar Setup dialog box appears, shown in Figure 8.3.

5. Click the Next button to continue.

6. Select the check box to accept the license agreement and click the Next button.

7. Accept the default installation folder and click the Install button. Alternatively, click the Browse button to select another folder.

8. A warning dialog box prompts you to close all open Internet Explorer windows. Do so, and click the Yes button to continue.

9. Select the Launch Internet Explorer with LinkedIn Toolbar check box and click the Finish button.

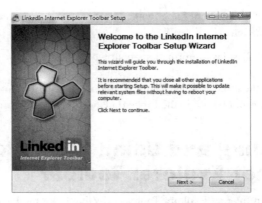

FIGURE 8.3   Setting up the LinkedIn Internet Explorer Toolbar.

Internet Explorer opens with the toolbar installed, shown in Figure 8.4.

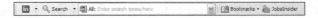

FIGURE 8.4   Search, access, and bookmark pages from LinkedIn while using Internet Explorer.

NOTE: **Where Is the LinkedIn Toolbar?**

If the LinkedIn toolbar doesn't appear, select View, Toolbars, LinkedIn Toolbar from the browser menu. Also verify that you meet the system requirements to install the toolbar.

Click the down arrow to the right of the LinkedIn button on your browser toolbar to display a drop-down list of options. These include

- ▶ **LinkedIn Home**. Takes you to LinkedIn's home page. This section also includes direct links to Find People, Find Jobs, Find Services, My Profile, and My Contacts.

- ▶ **Preferences**. Opens the Preferences dialog box, shown in Figure 8.5, in which you can enter your LinkedIn account information, specify when to open the JobsInsider, and activate the InfoBox in Web email option.

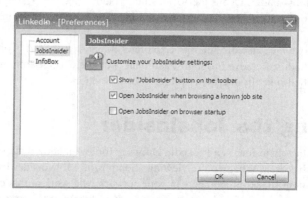

FIGURE 8.5   Specify your JobsInsider preferences in this dialog box.

▶ **Help**. Opens a help file where you can search for more information.

▶ **Check for Update**. Checks to see if there is a more recent version of the toolbar.

▶ **About**. Displays information about the toolbar.

The LinkedIn Toolbar also includes the following buttons:

▶ **Search.** Click the down arrow to the right of the search button to select search options. Options include all keywords, name, title, current title, company, current company, and jobs. Enter your search term and click the Search button to display relevant results in LinkedIn. You can also select the Clear Search History menu to clear your searches or the Advanced Search option to open the Advanced Search page in LinkedIn.

▶ **Bookmarks.** Click the Bookmark This page menu option to bookmark an active LinkedIn page. This option is available only if you're viewing a LinkedIn page that you can bookmark, such as a profile, search results, or a job listing. Select the Manage Bookmarks to open the Bookmarks window.

▶ **JobsInsider.** Opens the JobsInsider window. See the "Using the JobsInsider" section later in this lesson for more information.

To remove the LinkedIn Internet Explorer Toolbar, select Start, Control Panel, Add or Remove Programs, and then click the Change/Remove button in the LinkedIn Internet Explorer Toolbar section.

Using the JobsInsider

LinkedIn JobsInsider is a LinkedIn Browser Toolbar feature that assists in your job search. When you're viewing a job posting, JobsInsider lets you know about LinkedIn members in your network who work at that company and are potential inside connections for you. JobsInsider works with job postings on sites such as Monster, CareerBuilder, HotJobs, Craigslist, Simply Hired, Dice, or Vault.

> NOTE: **You Must Install the LinkedIn Browser Toolbar to Use JobsInsider**
>
> If you haven't installed the LinkedIn Browser Toolbar yet, click the JobsInsider link on the bottom navigation menu for installation instructions. See the "Installing and Using the LinkedIn Firefox Browser Toolbar" section and the "Installing and Using the LinkedIn Firefox Browser Toolbar" section earlier in this lesson for more information.

For example, if you're searching Monster.com for potential jobs, JobsInsider opens automatically, detecting that you're searching a job site. Figure 8.6 shows a sample view of JobsInsider.

When you open a job posting, JobsInsider lists the names of your first degree connections and includes links to their LinkedIn profiles. It also tells you the total people in your network who work at this company. Click the number to view a list of these people.

FIGURE 8.6   JobsInsider points out your inside connections at a hiring company.

NOTE: **You Can Activate and Deactivate JobsInsider**

To specify JobsInsider settings, click the LinkedIn button on your browser toolbar and select Preferences from the menu. In the Preferences dialog box, you can specify if you want to open JobsInsider when browsing a known job site, open upon browser startup, or not open at all.

Using the Outlook Toolbar

With the Outlook Toolbar, you can manage your LinkedIn network from within Microsoft Outlook. The toolbar requires that you run Windows XP or Vista and use Microsoft Outlook XP (2002), 2003, or 2007.

To install the Outlook Toolbar, close Outlook and follow these steps:

1. Click the Outlook Toolbar link on the bottom navigation menu. The LinkedIn Outlook Toolbar page.

2. Click the Download It Now button.

3. Click the OK button to confirm that you are located in one of the countries listed in the pop-up box.

4. Click Run to run the file. The LinkedIn Outlook Toolbar Setup dialog box opens.

5. Click the Next button to continue.

6. Select the check box to accept the license agreement and click the Next button.

7. Accept the default installation folder and click the Install button. Alternatively, click the Browse button to select another folder.

8. Select the Launch Microsoft Outlook with LinkedIn Outlook Toolbar check box and click the Finish button.

The LinkedIn toolbar and menu now appear in Outlook. The toolbar enables you to

▶ Receive suggestions about who to connect with on LinkedIn based on email frequency

▶ Send LinkedIn invitations with one click

▶ Update Outlook based on LinkedIn profile data

▶ Get notified when your contacts update their LinkedIn profiles

▶ Stay current with your network using the LinkedIn dashboard

▶ Search and access LinkedIn data from Outlook

NOTE: **Troubleshooting the Outlook Toolbar**

The installation of the Outlook Toolbar might require different steps based on your browser, operating system, and configuration. Refer to LinkedIn's online help for the latest news on toolbar updates and changes.

Creating an Email Signature

LinkedIn enables you to create an email signature that includes links to your profile and other popular LinkedIn features. You can use your LinkedIn email signature with popular email systems such as Microsoft Outlook, Outlook Express, Mozilla Thunderbird, and Yahoo! Mail.

To create an email signature, follow these steps:

1. Click the Overview link on the bottom navigation menu.

2. In the Email Signature section of the LinkedIn Tools page, click the Try It Now button. The Create Email Signature page opens, shown in Figure 8.7.

FIGURE 8.7   Create an email signature you can use with many popular email systems.

3. Select a layout for your email signature from the drop-down list. A preview of your signature with the selected layout appears on the page. To view all the options at once, click the View Gallery link.

4. Enter the contact information you want to appear on your signature in the Business Information, Contact Information, and Work Address sections.

5. If you want to include a company logo or your photo, enter the image's URL in the Image Selection field. Your image must be in the GIF, JPG, or PNG format; no larger than 50k; and no larger than 100 × 60 in size. To use your LinkedIn photo, right-click the photo on your profile and choose Copy Image Location or Copy Shortcut from the menu. (The menu option varies by browser.) Paste (Ctrl+V) this link in the Image Selection field.

NOTE: **You Can Link Only to an Image Already on the Web**
You must link to an image that already appears on the web, such as your LinkedIn photo or an image on your own website or blog. You can't upload an image.

---

6. Select any or all of the following options to place links on your email signature:

- ▶ Professional Profile link

- ▶ See Who We Know in Common link

- ▶ We're Hiring Link

7. Click the Click Here for Instructions link to save your signature. A new window opens, shown in Figure 8.8.

8. Copy your signature code by clicking in the text box and pressing Ctrl+C on your keyboard.

9. Select your email client from the drop-down list. Instructions for using the email signature in your email system appear.

10. Click the Close This Window link to close the window and install your new email signature.

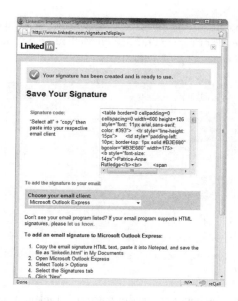

FIGURE 8.8 Copy and paste the code for your new email signature into your email system.

Using the Google Toolbar Assistant

The Google Toolbar Assistant optimizes the Google Toolbar by installing a LinkedIn search button. You need to the Google Toolbar (http://toolbar.google.com) for Firefox or Internet Explorer to use this feature.

To install the Google Toolbar Assistant, follow these steps:

1. Click the Overview link on the bottom navigation menu.

2. In the Google Toolbar section of the LinkedIn Tools page, click the Download It Now button. The Google Toolbar Custom Button Installer dialog box opens. If you haven't installed the Google Toolbar yet, you're prompted to do so before continuing.

3. Click the Add button.

4. In the dialog box that opens, specify whether you want to search by keywords or name in the Search Method field. You can change this later (see Figure 8.9).

FIGURE 8.9 Specify a search method for the LinkedIn button on the Google Toolbar.

5. Click the OK button. LinkedIn places the LinkedIn search button on the Google Toolbar (see Figure 8.10).

LinkedIn button

FIGURE 8.10 Quickly search for information on LinkedIn.

To use the search button, enter a search term in the text box and click the LinkedIn button. LinkedIn displays results based on the type of search method you specified (either a keyword or a name).

To change your search method or remove the search button, right-click the LinkedIn button and select LinkedIn Button Options from the menu.

Summary

In this lesson, you learned how to install and use tools that help you integrate LinkedIn with other popular websites and software programs.

LESSON 9

Finding a Job

In this lesson, you'll learn how to use LinkedIn as an effective job search tool, find and apply to job postings, and use LinkedIn's many other features for jobseekers.

Attracting Recruiters and Hiring Managers

LinkedIn is an excellent tool for jobseekers, but you need to create a stellar profile and develop a solid network if you want to maximize your results. Here are seven tips for making the most of LinkedIn as a job search tool.

- ▶ Complete your profile. LinkedIn reports that members with a complete profile generate 40 times more opportunities than those whose profiles aren't complete.

- ▶ Develop a solid network of connections. Your ability to use job search features such as JobsInsider or Inside Connections depends on having a reasonable number of connections. You should aim for at least 50 connections to maximize the benefits of these features, although they do work with fewer connections.

- ▶ Get recommendations. A complete profile includes at least three recommendations. Aim for recommendations from managers, executives, or actual clients. Peer recommendations, particularly those that you "trade" with colleagues by recommending each other, carry far less weight.

- ▶ Include keywords that are relevant to your profession and industry, such as skills, certifications, and degrees. Recruiters search for these words, and your profile should include them if you want to be found.

▶ Focus on results, not a list of duties. Remember that your profile is a concise summary of your qualifications, not a resume. (Although you can attach one if you like.) Emphasize your results and accomplishments; don't just list tasks you performed.

▶ Post a resume or portfolio. Using LinkedIn applications such as Box.net Files, you can attach PDFs to your profile.

▶ Indicate on your profile that you're seeking employment. If you're unemployed, include this information in your status, professional headline, or summary. Don't sound desperate, but do let your network know that you're looking for opportunities.

See Lesson 2, "Creating Your Profile," and Lesson 10, "Requesting and Providing Recommendations," for more information.

TIP: **Clean Up Your Digital Dirt Before Your Job Search**

Keep in mind that many recruiters now search the web for background information on potential candidates. It isn't enough to have a professional presence on LinkedIn. Review any other social networking profiles you have to ensure they also reinforce your professional image. If not, remove your "digital dirt" before you begin your job search. Also, verify that your contacts don't post photos or other content about you that would compromise your professional reputation.

Searching Job Postings

LinkedIn offers a large database of job postings that are posted directly on LinkedIn and on its partner site, Simply Hired.

TIP: **LinkedIn Offers Other Ways to Find Job Postings**

Although the Jobs page is LinkedIn's primary job search tool, you should also search the Jobs Discussion Board for any group you belong to and the Jobs box on the company profiles for your target employers. To do a quick search for jobs, use the search box on the top navigation menu.

To search job postings on LinkedIn, follow these steps:

1. Click the Jobs link on the top navigation menu. The Jobs page opens, shown in Figure 9.1.

FIGURE 9.1   Searching for jobs by keyword.

2. In the Find a Job Using Your LinkedIn Network box, enter Keywords related to your job search. For example, you could enter a job title, a job skill, or the name of a target company.

3. Select the Country you want to search.

4. If applicable, specify a Postal Code to narrow your job search. Leave this field blank to search for jobs nationwide.

5. Click the Search button. The Job Search Results page opens, shown in Figure 9.2.

The first tab, LinkedIn Jobs, lists jobs advertised on LinkedIn. On this tab, you can

▶ Sort jobs by clicking the Title, Company, Location, Date, or Posted By headings.

▶ Identify jobs that are listed exclusively on LinkedIn (denoted by the blue starburst icon).

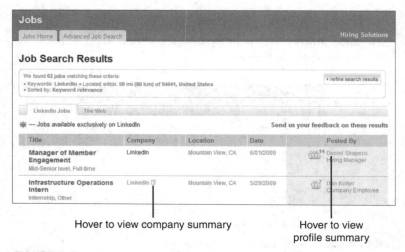

FIGURE 9.2   Viewing a list of jobs that match your criteria.

▶ Learn more about the companies that post jobs by hovering your mouse over the company name to open a pop-up with a brief summary of the company (if the company includes the company profile icon to the right of its name; if it doesn't, then this information isn't available). Click the View Profile link to open that company's complete profile.

▶ Learn more about the job poster by hovering your mouse over the name of the job poster to open a pop-up with a brief summary. Click the View Profile link to open the person's profile. If no name appears in this field, the company has chosen not to disclose this information.

▶ Learn more about the job posting (including a job description and application information) by clicking the job title.

The second tab, The Web, lists jobs advertised on the job search site Simply Hired. The format for job listings is similar to the LinkedIn Jobs tab but includes a JobsInsider link for each job. JobsInsider lists the people who work at that hiring company, highlighting those who are in your network. You can also install a JobsInsider toolbar to use when searching popular job sites. See Lesson 8, "Using LinkedIn Tools," for more information about the JobsInsider toolbar.

Click the Who Do I Know at [Company Name] link to view a list of people in your network who work at this company.

Viewing Job Postings

The content listed on a job posting varies according to what the hiring company chooses to display. The content that you see will also vary according to what type of connection you have to the poster and the connections you have to the people working at that company. A job posting (see Figure 9.3) might include some or all of the following features:

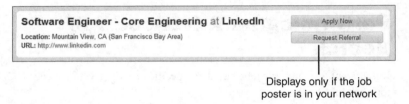

Displays only if the job
poster is in your network

FIGURE 9.3 Viewing a list of jobs that match specified criteria.

- ► A header listing the job title, location, and company URL.

- ► A detailed job description.

- ► The Forward This Job to a Friend link. Click to send a message to a connection who might be interested in this job.

- ► The Apply Now button. Click this button to apply for the job from LinkedIn. See the "Applying for a Job" section later in this lesson for more information.

- ► The Request Referral button. Click this button to open the Introductions page where you can request an introduction to the job poster. You can request introductions only to job posters in your network. Otherwise, the Request Referral button doesn't appear. See Lesson 6, "Communicating with Other LinkedIn Members," for more information about LinkedIn introductions.

▶ The Posted By box with a link to the job poster's LinkedIn profile and recommendations. A connection icon appears if this person is in your network. For example, if a job poster is connected
to one of your connections, the 2nd degree connection icon
appears. Click the See Who Connects You link to open this person's profile. On the profile, the How You're Connected to [First
Name] box lists all mutual connections.

▶ The Inside Connections to the Company box. Click one of the
links in this box to display the LinkedIn members in your network who work at this company. These people could provide
you inside information about potential job opportunities at the
company.

Performing an Advanced Job Search

If you want to search for jobs based on specific criteria, try an advanced
job search:

1. Click the down arrow next to the Jobs link on the top navigation
menu and select Advanced Job Search from the drop-down list.
You can also open this page by clicking the Advanced Job
Search tab on the main Jobs page or by clicking the Advanced
link when searching for jobs from the search box on the top navigation menu. Figure 9.4 shows the Advanced Job Search page.

2. In the Search For text box, enter keywords (such as a job title, a
skill, or a certification). See Lesson 7, "Searching on LinkedIn,"
for more information on using advanced search criteria.

3. Specify the criteria for your search. Options include the following:

▶ Location

▶ Experience Level (ranging from executive jobs to intern-
ships)

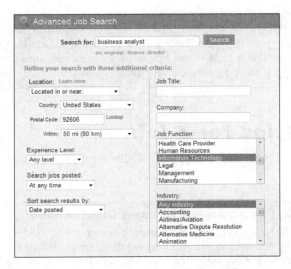

FIGURE 9.4   Performing an advanced job search.

▶ Search Jobs Posted (the date the job was posted, such as in the last day or at any time)

▶ Sort Search Results By (specific criteria such as date posted or location)

▶ Job Title

▶ Company name

▶ Job Function (such as Accounting/Auditing, Engineering, Finance, Information Technology, Marketing, and so forth)

▶ Industry (such as Banking, Biotechnology, Computer Software, Insurance, Real Estate, and so forth)

4. Click the Search button to display job search results.

See the previous section, "Searching Job Postings," for more information about the Job Search Results page.

TIP: **Specify Only the Most Important Criteria**

You don't need to specify criteria in all the fields available on the Advanced Search page. Start with a few choices and then narrow or expand your search based on your search results.

Applying for a Job

You can apply for a job posted on LinkedIn directly from the job description.

NOTE: **Not All Job Application Pages Look the Same**

Although the job application process is similar for all jobs, the form you complete isn't identical for every job you apply for on LinkedIn. In addition, clicking a job title from The Web tab takes you to the Simply Hired website (www.simplyhired.com).

To apply for a job from a LinkedIn posting, following these steps:

1. In the job description for the job you would like to apply for, click the Apply Now button and an application page will display. Figure 9.5 shows a sample application page.

2. In the Write Cover Letter text box, enter your cover letter. A good cover letter summarizes strengths and accomplishments that are relevant to this job.

3. In the Enter Contact Information section, enter details about your name, email address, and contact information.

4. Click the Browse button in the Upload Resume section to upload your resume as a text file, Word document, PDF, or HTML file of no more than 200k. LinkedIn attaches your uploaded resume in its original format.

5. Preview your profile in the Review Profile section. Make any necessary changes before submitting your application.

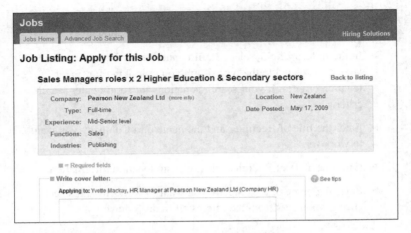

FIGURE 9.5 Applying for jobs directly from LinkedIn.

6. Click the Next button.

7. Review and confirm your application one more time before submitting. Be sure to check for spelling, grammar, and content.

8. Click the Submit Application button to submit your application for the job.

Finding Recruiters and Hiring Managers

The good news for jobseekers: Thousands of recruiters and hiring managers maintain profiles on LinkedIn. To find them, select Search People in the quick search box on the top navigation menu. Then click the Advanced link to the right of the box to open the Advanced Search page.

There are several ways to find recruiters and hiring managers on the Advanced Search page. Some examples include the following:

▶ In the Industry field, select Staffing and Recruiting and enter keywords related to the type of job you're looking for. Enter location criteria. If your search is nationwide, don't enter search criteria.

▶ Enter the title of Recruiter and the name of a Company you want to work for.

▶ Enter the Title of Recruiter plus relevant location information.

▶ Enter the name of a Company you want to work for and select Hiring Managers from the Interested In drop-down list.

Searching for appropriate contacts is a combination of art and science, so you might need to revise your search criteria several times before you find the appropriate people.

CAUTION: **Don't Spam Recruiters and Hiring Managers**

Remember that LinkedIn is a networking and research tool, not a means of spamming prospective recruiters and employers. When you do find good targets for your job search, review their profiles carefully to determine the best way to contact them. Some recruiters provide links to external sites for job candidates. If your target is a hiring manager, determine whether you can reach this person through a network introduction. Alternatively, consider sending a brief message to hiring managers who indicate they are open to job inquiries.

Summary

In this lesson, you learned about LinkedIn's many job search tools. In addition, you learned the most effective way to conduct a job search on LinkedIn.

LESSON 10

Requesting and Providing Recommendations

In this lesson, you'll learn how to request, provide, manage, and revise professional recommendations on LinkedIn.

Understanding LinkedIn Recommendations

LinkedIn enables you to request recommendations from and provide recommendations to the people in your professional network. Recommendations are a powerful networking tool, so consider carefully whom you want to ask for a recommendation and whom you want to recommend as part of your overall LinkedIn strategy.

LinkedIn offers four types of recommendations:

- ▶ **Colleague**. You worked with this person at the same company as a manager, peer, or employee.
- ▶ **Business Partner**. You worked with this person in another capacity, not as a colleague or client. For example, you worked at partner companies, performed volunteer or association work together, and so forth.
- ▶ **Student**. You were a teacher, advisor, or fellow student at the same school.
- ▶ **Service Provider**. You hired this person to perform services. Service Provider recommendations differ from the other recommendation types in that they also appear in the LinkedIn Service

Providers directory. See Lesson 14, "Using LinkedIn Service Providers," for more information about service provider recommendations.

The recommendation process involves several steps between two people to ensure that both approve the recommendation before it is final. For example, if Anne wants to request a recommendation from her former manager, Sophie—a common type of request—the process requires four steps:

- ▶ **Step 1**. Anne sends a recommendation request to Sophie.

- ▶ **Step 2**. Sophie receives the request and submits a recommendation for Anne.

- ▶ **Step 3**. Anne receives a notification about Sophie's recommendation and accepts the recommendation.

- ▶ **Step 4**. LinkedIn displays the recommendation on Anne's profile.

Obviously, this process assumes that both Anne and Sophie approve each step. LinkedIn also offers options for you to request clarifications and changes. If you write an unsolicited recommendation for a connection without receiving a recommendation request, your process starts at step 2 with submitting the recommendation.

Requesting Recommendations

Receiving recommendations from managers, colleagues, and clients can help you achieve your networking goals on LinkedIn. LinkedIn suggests that a complete profile should include at least three recommendations for maximum effectiveness.

Before you send your requests, however, think about what you want to achieve. Be clear about your goals so that your connections write recommendations that help you achieve them. For example, if you want to move into a management position, you should request a recommendation that discusses your leadership abilities. If you want to change careers, emphasize crossover skills.

TIP: **Let Your Connections Know You Want a Recommendation**

Although LinkedIn notifies your connections that you've requested a recommendation, it's a good idea that this message doesn't come as a surprise. Talk to the people you want to recommend you so that they're aware of your request and know what to emphasize in their recommendation.

To request a recommendation from one of your connections, follow these steps:

1. Click the Recommendations link on the expanded left navigation menu. The Received Recommendations page opens, shown in Figure 10.1.

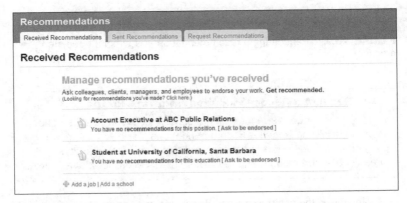

FIGURE 10.1   Asking your connections for professional recommendations.

2. Click the Ask to Be Endorsed link next to the related position or school. The Request Recommendations page opens, shown in Figure 10.2.

TIP: **Keep Your Profile Up-to-Date**

The Received Recommendations page displays only positions and schools you've already entered on your profile. If you haven't done this, click the Add a Job or Add a School link to complete this step first.

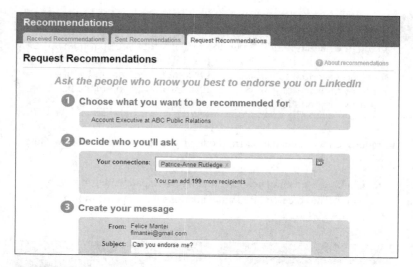

FIGURE 10.2   Requesting a recommendation is a simple, three-step process.

NOTE: **Request a Recommendation from Your Profile**

You can also request a recommendation on the Edit My Profile page. To do so, click the Request Recommendations link below the related position or school in the Experience or Education section. If you already have one recommendation, this link is called the Manage link.

---

3. In step 1, the position or school you selected appears by default. To change this, return to the previous page.

4. In step 2, start typing the name of the connection you want to ask for a recommendation. Select the correct name from the drop-down list of options that appear.

CAUTION: **Don't Mass Produce Recommendation Requests**

Although you can request a recommendation from up to 200 connections at a time, it's a much better practice to personalize each recommendation request you send. If you really want to send your request to more than one person, however, click the View All Connections button to select your recipients.

5. In step 3, create your message asking for a recommendation. LinkedIn provides sample text for you, but you should customize this for each request. Be specific and let your connection know what you want to achieve with this recommendation. You don't need to add a salutation; LinkedIn does this automatically.

6. Click the Send button. LinkedIn sends your recommendation request to its target recipient. If you selected more than one person in step 2, each person receives an individual message.

See "Responding to Recommendation Requests," to learn what happens when a connection receives your recommendation request.

Managing Recommendation Requests

After you send a recommendation request, the Received Recommendations tab indicates that you have a pending request (see Figure 10.3). This text remains until your connection submits a recommendation for you.

To review your request, click the Manage link below the related position or school. The Manage Received Recommendations page opens, shown in Figure 10.4.

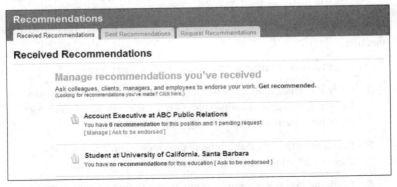

FIGURE 10.3   Monitoring your pending recommendation requests.

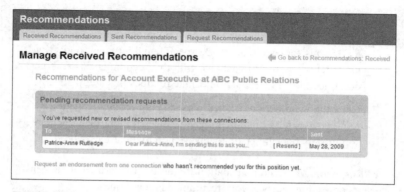

FIGURE 10.4   Re-send requests that have been pending for more than a week.

On this page, you can view a list of the recommendations you've requested and the date you requested them. If your request has been pending for more than a week, click the Resend link to send your request again with a message to the recipient. It's also a good idea to contact this person directly.

Responding to Recommendation Requests

LinkedIn sends a message to your Inbox when you receive recommendation requests. The default subject line for these messages is "Can You Endorse Me?" unless the person requesting the recommendation modified this text.

To respond to a recommendation request, follow these steps:

1. Click the Inbox link on your expanded left navigation menu. See Lesson 6, "Communicating with Other LinkedIn Members," for more information about working with your Inbox.

2. Select the message that contains the recommendation request. Figure 10.5 illustrates a sample recommendation request.

3. Click the Write Recommendation button to write your recommendation. The Select Type page opens, shown in Figure 10.6.

FIGURE 10.5   LinkedIn notifies you every time you receive a recommendation request.

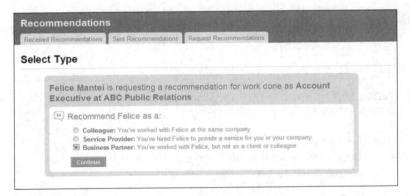

FIGURE 10.6   Your options vary depending on the recommendation type you choose.

NOTE: **LinkedIn Handles Student Requests Differently**

If this is for a student request, LinkedIn doesn't ask you to select a recommendation type and opens the Create Your Recommendation page directly.

4. If this recommendation is for a position, select from the following options: Colleague, Service Provider, or Business Partner. See "Understanding LinkedIn Recommendations," earlier in this lesson for more information about these recommendation types.

5. Click the Continue button to open the Create Your Recommendation page, shown in Figure 10.7.

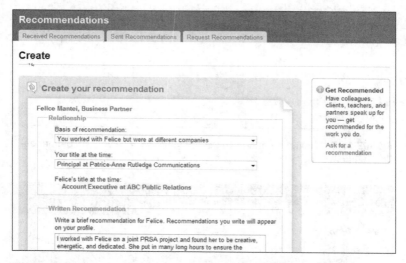

FIGURE 10.7   Create a recommendation that describes this person's accomplishments clearly and concisely.

6. Select a Basis of Recommendation from the drop-down list. Depending on the type of recommendation you're giving these options could include

> ▶ **Colleague**. Specify whether you managed this person; reported to this person; were senior to this person, but didn't manage this person directly; held a lower position, but didn't report to this person; worked in the same group; or worked in different groups.

> ▶ **Business Partner**. Specify whether you worked together at different companies or whether the person was your client.

    ▶ **Student**. Specify whether you were a teacher, advisor, or fellow student.

7. Select Your Title at the Time from the drop-down list, which includes the positions on your profile.

8. Enter your recommendation in the Written Recommendation box. Write a concise, specific recommendation that relates to the position and the goals of the person you're recommending.

9. Click the View/Edit button to display the Personalize This Message text box, where you can personalize the message you send to the person requesting your recommendation. This text doesn't appear on the recommendation itself.

10. Click the Send button to send the recommendation and accompanying message to the requestor.

TIP: **Consider Carefully Who You Recommend**

Consider carefully before recommending someone on LinkedIn. Remember that your reputation is based not only on who recommends you, but also on who you recommend. Is this someone you would recommend in the real world? If not, reply privately to the person explaining that you don't feel comfortable giving the recommendation. For example, you might not know the person well enough for a recommendation, or your experience working together might not have been a positive one.

Making a Recommendation

At times, you might want to recommend your connections even if they don't send you a recommendation request. To make a recommendation, follow these steps:

1. Click the Recommendations link on the expanded left navigation menu.

2. Scroll down the Received Recommendations page to the Make a Recommendation box, shown in Figure 10.8.

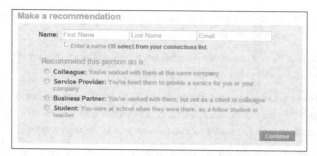

FIGURE 10.8   You can make several kinds of recommendations on LinkedIn.

> TIP: **Make Recommendations from a Connection's Profile Page**
>
> Another way to initiate a recommendation is to visit a connection's profile page and click the Recommend link below the related position or school, which opens the Create Your Recommendation page.

3. Click the Select from Your Connections List link to select your target recipient. Alternatively, enter a person's name and email address.

4. Select the type of recommendation you want to write. Options include Colleague, Service Provider, Business Partner, or Student. See Lesson 14 for more information about service provider recommendations.

5. Click the Continue button to open the Create Your Recommendation page.

See "Responding to Recommendation Requests," earlier in this lesson for more information on completing the Create Your Recommendation page. The process is the same whether you respond to a recommendation request or initiate it yourself.

Accepting Recommendations

When someone recommends you, LinkedIn sends you a notification message (see Figure 10.9). If you indicate that you want to receive email notifications on the Account & Settings page, LinkedIn also notifies you by email.

Open the message to view the complete recommendation. Figure 10.10 illustrates a sample message.

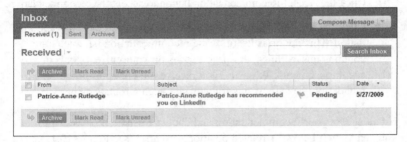

FIGURE 10.9 LinkedIn notifies you when one of your connections recommends you.

FIGURE 10.10 Review your recommendation for accuracy before accepting it.

On this page, you can:

▶ Select Show This Recommendation on My Profile if you want to display the recommendation.

▶ Select Hide This Recommendation on My Profile if you want to hide the recommendation. In general, displaying your recommendations is a good promotional tool. You should hide unsolicited recommendations you don't want others to view.

▶ Click the Accept Recommendation button to accept the recommendation.

▶ Click the Request Replacement button to ask for a revised recommendation. This option is useful if the recommendation isn't accurate, contains misspellings, or doesn't focus on your current goals or accomplishments. To ensure you receive a more appropriate recommendation, be sure to specify *why* you need a replacement.

If you accept your recommendation and choose to show it on your profile, you can view it below its related position or school (see Figure 10.11).

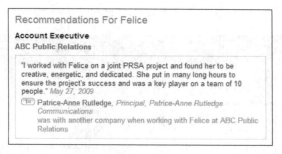

FIGURE 10.11   View accepted recommendations on your profile.

Managing Received Recommendations

Several times a year, you should review your recommendations to verify that they're still relevant to your current goals. You might want to hide a recommendation that's no longer relevant or request updated recommendations from those who have recommended you in the past.

To manage your recommendations, click the Recommendations link on the expanded left navigation menu.

On the Received Recommendations page, click the Manage link below the recommendation you want to change. The Manage Received Recommendations page opens, shown in Figure 10.12.

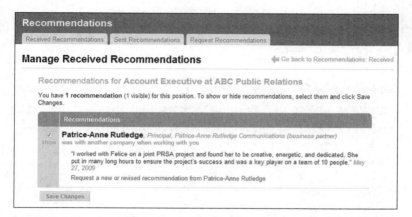

FIGURE 10.12   Review your recommendations regularly to verify that they still meet your needs.

To hide a recommendation from your profile, remove the check mark next to the Show check box. Click the Save Changes button to save this change.

To ask a connection for a revised recommendation, click the Request a New or Revised Recommendation From [name] link. LinkedIn sends a message to this connection asking for a revision. Be sure to communicate clearly what you're looking for in your revised recommendation. For example, you might want to revise a recommendation if your job duties for the same position have changed or you want to emphasize a different aspect of your job for future career growth.

TIP: **Request a New Recommendation if You Have a New Job Title**

If you receive a promotion or have a new job title, add a new position and request a recommendation for that job rather than revise an existing recommendation.

Managing Sent Recommendations

To manage the recommendations you give others, click the Recommendations link on the expanded left navigation menu. Click the Sent Recommendations tab to open the Sent Recommendations page, shown in Figure 10.13.

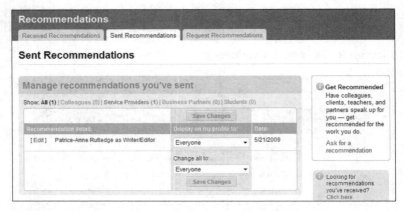

FIGURE 10.13   Revise or withdraw a recommendation on the Sent Recommendations page.

On this page, you can

▶ Change the display options for a recommendation. By default, the recommendations you give your connections appear on your profile for all LinkedIn members to see. Click the Display on My Profile To drop-down list, and choose either Connections Only or No One to change this.

▶ Revise a recommendation. Click the Edit link next to the recommendation you want to revise and make your changes on the Edit Your Recommendation page. Click the Send button to make your changes and notify your connection.

▶ Withdraw a recommendation. Click the Click the Edit link next to the recommendation you want to withdraw. On the Edit Your Recommendation page, click the Withdraw This Recommendation link. A pop-up box asks you to confirm that you want to withdraw the recommendation.

Summary

In this lesson, you learned how to request, provide, and manage professional recommendations on LinkedIn.

Working with LinkedIn Groups

In this lesson, you'll learn how to participate on LinkedIn Groups, manage your groups, and create your own group.

Understanding LinkedIn Groups

LinkedIn Groups offer a way for like-minded individuals to share and discuss relevant topics related to the focus of the group. With LinkedIn Groups, you can network and share ideas with industry peers, discover job leads and recruit quality talent, promote your career or business, and learn about a wide range of professional topics.

Remember, to maximize the publicity potential of LinkedIn Groups, focus on visibility and sharing your expertise rather than overt sales or advertising.

LinkedIn Groups take many forms. There are groups for alumni, associations, non-profits, professional interests, corporations, general networking, conference attendees, and personal interests. Your group activity appears on the Group Updates section on your home page, providing additional visibility for your group actions and your groups.

LinkedIn imposes a limit of 50 group memberships per account holder. If you reach 50 groups and want to join another, you need to leave an existing group. Because of this limit, it's important to consider carefully which groups will provide you with the most value and help you meet your goals.

Joining a Group

One of the best ways to find a group to join is to search LinkedIn's Groups Directory. To search the directory for potential groups to join, follow these steps:

1. Click the Groups link on the left navigation menu to open the My Groups page.

2. Click the Find a Group button. The Featured Groups page opens, shown in Figure 11.1.

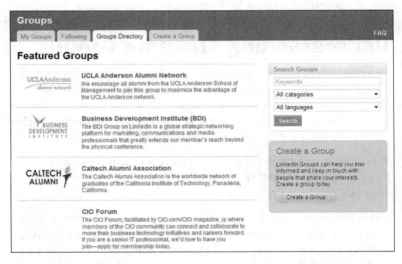

FIGURE 11.1   Join a featured group or search for one that meets your criteria.

3. In the Search Groups box, enter keywords related to the group you want to find. For example, you could enter the name of a company, school, professional association, skill, or hobby.

4. If you want to narrow your search results by category, click All Categories and select a category from the drop-down list.

Options include groups for professional association members, alumni, corporate employees, conference attendees, non-profits, and general networking.

5. If you want to narrow your search by language, click All Languages and select a language from the drop-down list.

6. Click the Search button to open the Search Results page, which displays a preview of each group that matches your search criteria. The preview boxes include a group description, the group owner's name, and the number of members. Click the group title to view more details, including a list of people in your network who already belong to this group.

NOTE: **Open Groups Versus Restricted Groups**

Although most groups are open to all LinkedIn members, be sure to clarify this in the group's description. Some groups, for example, require you to be an alumnus of a school or company or a paid member of a professional association.

---

7. Click the Join This Group link on the Search Results page to open the Join Group page, as shown in Figure 11.2.

8. If you want the group logo to appear in the Groups section on your profile, select the Group Logo check box. Placing this logo on your profile identifies you to fellow members.

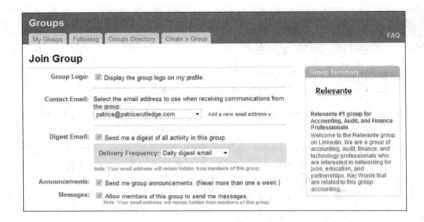

FIGURE 11.2   Select your group contact preferences on the Join Group page.

9. Specify the Contact Email for sending group announcements and updates.

10. If you want to receive email updates of group activity, select the Digest Email check box. You can choose to have updates delivered on a daily basis or a weekly basis.

NOTE: **View Group Updates Online**

If you don't want to receive email notifications, you can keep up with your groups on LinkedIn. Your home page displays group updates, and the Updates tab on each group's page summarizes the latest activity as well.

---

11. To receive group announcements no more than once per week, select the Announcements check box.

12. To allow other members of your group to send you messages on LinkedIn, select the Messages check box. (They won't see your personal email address.)

13. Click the Join Group button to join the group.

The My Groups page opens, which lists your current and pending groups. Group managers approve join requests manually unless the group was set up for automatic approval. Your status for a new group on the My Groups page is listed as pending approval. This status remains until the group manager approves you. If you want to follow up with the group owner about a join request, click the Send Message to the Group Manager link. If want to cancel your request to join the group, click the Withdraw Request link.

Viewing Your Groups

You can view a list of the groups you belong to by clicking the Groups link on the expanded left navigation menu. The My Groups page opens, shown in Figure 11.3.

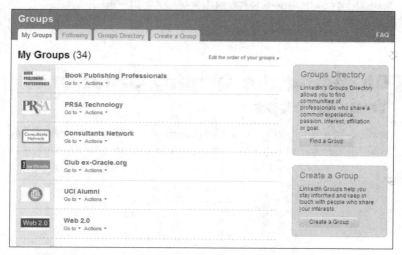

FIGURE 11.3   View information about all your groups in one place.

This page lists all your groups with the following links appearing below each group's name:

▶ **Go To**. Click the Go To link and select one of the following options from the drop-down list: Overview, Subgroups, Discussions, Jobs, News, Updates, Members, or Settings.

▶ **Actions**. Click the Actions link and select one of the following actions: Share, Start a Discussion, or Leave Group.

You'll learn more about accessing these group features later in this lesson.

If your request to join a group is still pending, you'll see a notification in that group's preview box. The links to specific tasks aren't available until you're approved for a group. If you are not yet approved, your options include emailing the group manager or withdrawing your request.

If you're the group manager, a Manage link is also available.

> TIP: **View Your Group Information on Your Profile**
> You can also view a list of the groups you belong to on your profile.

Changing the Display Order of Your Groups

For easy access to your groups, LinkedIn displays the first three groups in your My Groups list under the Groups link on the expanded left navigation menu (see Figure 11.4).

FIGURE 11.4   Access your favorite groups directly from your home page.

If you're a frequent participant in group activity, it's a good idea to display your favorite groups on this navigation menu. You can also increase the number of displayed groups from 3 to as many as 10.

To change the display order of your groups, follow these steps:

1. Click the Groups link on the expanded left navigation menu.

2. Scroll to the bottom of the My Groups page and click the Change the Display Order of Your Groups link. The Groups Order and Display page opens, shown in Figure 11.5.

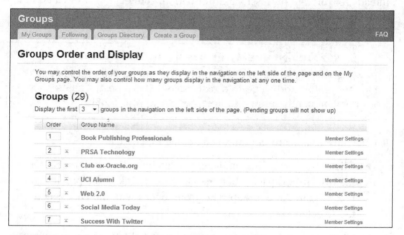

FIGURE 11.5   Choosing the order in which your groups appear.

3. Select the number of group links to display on the expanded left navigation menu. Options range from 1 to 10.

4. Use the Order field to move each of your groups up or down until you reach your desired display order.

> NOTE: **Change Your Settings for Each of Your Groups**
>
> You can specify different settings for each of your groups. Click the Member Settings link to make changes to a particular group. See "Managing Group Settings" later in this lesson for more information.

5. Click the Save Changes button to save your changes, which
   appear on the navigation menu.

Participating in Group Discussions

Participating in discussions is one of the greatest values of joining a
group. With LinkedIn Group Discussions, you can view discussion
threads for relevant professional information, add a comment to a current
discussion, or start your own discussion.

CAUTION: **Focus on Quality, Professional Discussions**

As with everything else on LinkedIn, focus on intelligent, meaningful
comments that add value to a discussion. Don't post a sales pitch
or irrelevant comment just to lead people to your profile.

To view discussions for a group you belong to, you can

▶ Click the Groups link on the expanded left navigation menu. On
   the My Groups page, click the Discussion link in the preview
   box of your target group. The group opens with the Discussion
   tab selected.

▶ Click the actual group link on the expanded left navigation menu
   or the group logo on your profile page. The group page opens
   with the Overview tab selected. This tab displays a summary of
   recent discussions, but you can click the Discussions tab to view
   additional discussions.

The Discussion tab displays a preview of the discussions with the most
recent activity. Each preview box includes the name and photo of the
person who started the discussion, when it was posted, a link to add

comments (plus the number of comments), and a link to follow the discussion.

Although Recent Activity is the default view for discussions, you can also click any of the links in the Discussions box on the left side of the page for additional views.

Adding Comments to a Discussion

To add a comment to a discussion, follow these steps:

1. Click the Add Comment link in the preview box of any discussion topic that appears on the Discussions tab. The Discussion page opens, displaying the original post and the comments of other LinkedIn members. If a comment already exists, this link displays the number of comments. For example, if two people posted comments, you will see the 2 Comments link instead of the Add Comment link.

2. Enter your own comment in the Add a Comment text box, shown in Figure 11.6.

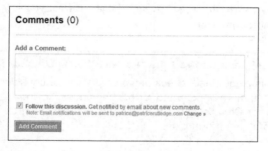

Comments (0)

Add a Comment:

☑ **Follow this discussion.** Get notified by email about new comments.
Note: Email notifications will be sent to patrice@patricerutledge.com Change »

Add Comment

FIGURE 11.6   Contributing your own thoughts to a discussion.

3. If you want to receive email notification of any new comments in this discussion, select the Follow This Discussion check box. You can also view all the group activity you're following by clicking the Following tab on the My Groups page.

4. Click the Add Comment button to post your comment.

TIP: **Reply Privately if You Don't Want to Post a Comment**

To reply privately to the original poster or anyone who posted a comment, click the Reply Privately link next to their name.

After you post a comment, LinkedIn gives you 15 minutes to revise it. Click the Edit Comment link below your comment to make any changes. Click the Delete Comment link to remove your comment from the discussion at any time.

Starting a Discussion

To start your own discussion, follow these steps:

1. Click the Start a Discussion link on the Discussions tab. The Start a Discussion page opens.

2. Enter a Topic or Question for discussion. To encourage participation, keep the topic or question brief and focused.

3. Enter Additional Details about your discussion topic. Do you want advice from other professionals? Are you seeking opinions on a newsworthy topic? Be specific about what you seek in member comments.

NOTE: **Post Jobs on the Jobs Tab, Not the Discussion Tab**

The Is This a Job Post? check box prompts you to consider whether your post is more appropriate for posting under the Jobs tab. See the "Using a Group's Jobs Discussion Board" section later in this lesson for more information.

4. If you want to receive email notification of any new comments in this discussion, select the Follow This Discussion check box.

5. Click the Submit for Discussion button to post your discussion topic to the Discussions tab where other members can view and comment on it.

Viewing and Submitting News Articles

Submitting links to news articles and commenting on them is another good way to participate in a group. A news article is a link to an external site such as a newspaper or magazine article or a blog post that's relevant to the topic of the group. For example, you could submit an article you just read in a major newspaper, or you could submit a great post from your favorite blog.

Submitting your own articles, blog posts, or media coverage is acceptable, but don't overdo this feature as a promotional tool. Submit only the most informative, meaningful content that offers value to the members of your group.

To view news articles for a group you belong to, you can

▶ Click the Groups link on the expanded left navigation menu. On the My Groups page, select Go To, News in the preview box of your target group. The group opens with the News tab selected.

▶ Click the actual group link on the expanded left navigation menu, or the group logo on your profile page to open the group page with the Overview tab selected. Click the News tab to view news articles.

The News tab displays a preview of the news articles with the most activity. Each preview box includes the name of the news source, when it was posted, the number of views, a link to discuss, and the number of discussion comments, if any. You can also hover over the news article title to open a pop-up box with more details, including a brief summary and the name and photo of the person who submitted the news item.

> NOTE: **Alert LinkedIn of Inappropriate Posts**
> If a news article is inappropriate, click the Flag Article As link in this pop-up box to alert the LinkedIn staff. Examples of articles to flag include spam or advertisements.

Although Most Activity is the default view for discussion, you can access additional views by clicking any of the links in the News box on the left side of the page.

To view the actual news article, click its title link on the News tab. LinkedIn opens the external news item in a shared window.

To exit LinkedIn and move to the external site, click the Close [x] button in the upper-right corner of the screen. To return to the News tab, click your browser's Back button.

To add a discussion comment to a news article, follow these steps:

1. Click the Discuss link below the news article preview on the News tab. The News Discussion page opens, displaying the original post and the comments of other LinkedIn members.

2. Enter your comment in the Add a Comment text box.

3. If you want to receive email notification of any new comments in this discussion, select the Follow This Discussion check box.

4. Click the Add Comment button to post your comment.

After you post a comment, LinkedIn gives you 15 minutes to revise it. Click the Edit Comment link below your comment to make any changes. Click the Delete Comment link to remove your comment from the discussion at any time.

To post a news article, follow these steps:

1. Click the Submit a New Article link on the News tab. The Submit a News Article pop-up box opens.

2. Enter the complete URL of the article you want to post.

3. Click the Continue button. Figure 11.7 shows the Submit and Share a News Article page.

4. LinkedIn suggests a Title for this article based on its original source, but you can edit this title if you want.

5. LinkedIn suggests an article Summary based on its original source. Again, you can edit this text to better reflect the article's content. LinkedIn displays only the first 250 characters.

6. Enter the news Source (such as the name of a newspaper, magazine, or blog).

7. In the Add Comment text box, let group members know why this article is relevant.

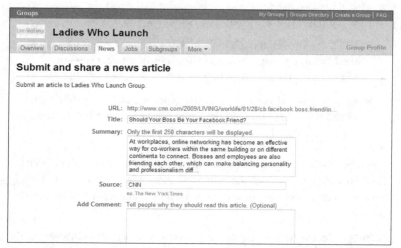

FIGURE 11.7   Submitting news articles to share with your fellow group members.

8. If you want to receive email notification of any new comments for this news article, select the Follow This Discussion check box.

9. Click the Add News Article button to post your article on the News tab where other members can view and comment on it.

Using a Group's Jobs Discussion Board

If you're recruiting for a position that would interest the members of a specific LinkedIn group, you can post your job on the group's Jobs Discussion Board, located on the Jobs tab. This is also a great place for jobseekers to find targeted jobs.

> TIP: **Consider LinkedIn's Other Job Search and Recruiting Tools**
>
> For more ways to search for and post jobs on LinkedIn, click the Jobs link on the top navigation menu. See Lesson 9, "Finding a Job," and Web Lesson 1, "Recruiting Job Candidates," for more information.

To view job postings for a group you belong to, you can

- ▶ Click the Groups link on the expanded left navigation menu. On the My Groups page, select Go To, Jobs in the preview box of your target group. The group opens with the Jobs tab selected.

- ▶ Click the actual group link on the expanded left navigation menu or the group logo on your profile to open the group page. Then, click the Jobs tab.

The Jobs tab displays a preview of the jobs with the most recent activity. Each preview box includes the name and photo of the person who posted the job, when it was posted, and links to add comments or follow a job's comments.

Although Recent Activity is the default view, you can also click any of the links in the Jobs box on the right side of the page for additional views.

To view the actual job posting, select the Jobs tab and click the job title link.

To add a comment to a job posting you're viewing, follow these steps:

1. Enter your comment in the Add a Comment text box at the bottom of the job detail page.

2. If you want to receive email notification of any new comments related to this job, select the Follow This Job check box.

3. Click the Add Comment button to post your comment.

> TIP: **Reply Privately if You Don't Want to Post a Comment**
>
> To reply privately to the original poster or anyone who posted a comment, click the Reply Privately link.

After you post a comment, LinkedIn gives you 15 minutes to revise it. Click the Edit Comment link below your comment to make any changes. Click the Delete Comment link to remove your comment from the discussion at any time.

To post a job, follow these steps:

1. Select the Jobs tab and click the Post a Job link. The Post a Job page opens, shown in Figure 11.8.

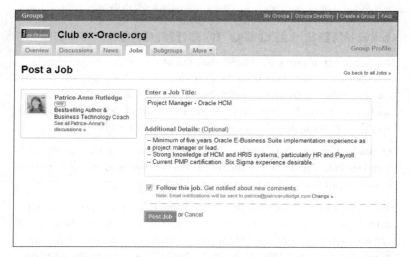

FIGURE 11.8   Post a job targeted to members of a specific LinkedIn group.

2. Enter a Job Title that clearly defines the nature of the job.

3. Enter Additional Details about your job. If you don't want potential candidates to contact you through LinkedIn, be sure to provide alternate contact information.

4. If you want to receive email notification of any new comments related to the job you post, select the Follow This Job check box.

5. Click the Post Job button to post your job to the Jobs tab.

Viewing Group Updates

To view the latest group updates, click the More tab on any group page
and then select Updates from the drop-down list. The Updates page lists
activity for the current and previous day, such as who joined the group,
who started a discussion, who posted comments, and so forth. The default
view is a summary. Click the Full View link to display more details. You
can also click the Last Week and Two Weeks Ago links to view prior
updates.

Viewing Group Members

To view a list of group members, click the More tab on any group page
and then select Members from the drop-down list. This page tells you how
many members a group has and displays previews of each group member,
starting with you. From there, LinkedIn lists your 1st degree connections,
your 2nd degree connections, and, finally, all other members.

Depending on members' settings and connection to you, their preview
could include a photo, a profile link, a professional headline, their number
of connections, and links to connect and send a message.

To search a group's member list for members matching specific criteria,
enter keywords in the Search Group box and click the Search button. You
can also search groups from the quick search box on the top navigation
menu. See Lesson 7, "Searching on LinkedIn," for more information on
searching for people.

Managing Group Settings

To revise your settings for a group, click the More tab on any group page
and then select My Settings from the drop-down list. The Settings page
opens, which gives you the option to modify the visibility and contact
options for a specific group.

The Settings page is identical to the Join a Group page. See "Joining a
Group," earlier in this lesson for more information on the settings you can
modify on this page.

Sharing Information About Groups

If you're a member of a particular group that you think your connections would also enjoy, let them know about it by selecting Actions, Share on the My Groups page. As a reminder, you can click the Groups link on the expanded left navigation menu to open this page.

LinkedIn takes you to your inbox where you can send a group link to as many as 50 of your connections. For best results, let your connections know why you recommend this group or why it's appropriate for them.

See Lesson 6, "Communicating with Other LinkedIn Members," for more information about the inbox and sending messages.

Leaving a Group

If you decide that a group no longer meets your needs or you have to pare down your current group membership to make room for new groups, you can easily leave a group.

To do so, select Action, Leave Group on the My Groups page. LinkedIn displays a pop-up box asking you to confirm that you want to leave the group. Click the Yes, Leave Group button to remove the group from your My Groups page.

Creating Your Own Group

Creating your own group is a good way to develop a community for a topic, profession, or interest. Before you create a group, consider the following:

- ▶ Is there already a similar group on LinkedIn Groups? If so, how will your group differ? What value will you add?

- ▶ Is your proposed group an advertisement in disguise? Although many LinkedIn members do benefit from their participation with LinkedIn Groups, you need to create a group whose focus is providing value and community to its members. If you don't, your group most likely won't succeed.

▶ Do you have the time to maintain and support your group? If you don't respond quickly to join requests and keep the activity going with your group, your group won't flourish.

To create a new LinkedIn group, follow these steps:

1. Click the Groups link on the expanded left navigation menu.

2. On the My Groups page, click the Create a Group button. The Create a Group page opens, shown in Figure 11.9.

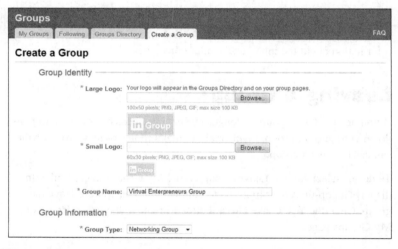

FIGURE 11.9   Creating your own group.

3. Click the Browse button to select and upload a Large Logo or a Small Logo. Large logos are 100×50 pixels; in the PNG, JPEG, or GIF format; and a maximum size of 100 KB. Small logos are 60×30 pixels with the same size limitations and format types.

4. Enter a Group Name. If your group also exists outside of LinkedIn, you can increase visibility by including the actual group name rather than just an acronym. For example, enter International Association of Business Communicators (IABC) instead of only IABC.

5. Select a Group Type. Options include alumni, corporate, conference, networking, nonprofit, professional, or other groups. The Other group type is most appropriate for special interest or hobby groups that don't fit into any other category.

6. Enter a Summary of your group. In this text box, indicate your group's focus, goals, and any membership benefits your group might provided for LinkedIn members. This summary appears in the Groups Directory.

7. In the Full Description text box, enter more details to display on your group pages.

8. If your group has an external website, enter the URL in the Website field.

9. Enter the Group Owner Email. LinkedIn sends all messages about your group to this email address.

10. In the Group Visibility section, indicate whether you want to list your group in the Groups Directory and allow group members to display your logo on their profiles. These options are great promotional tools for your group. Unless you have a specific need for privacy, it's a good idea to make your group visible.

11. Select the Group Access check box if you want LinkedIn to approve new group members automatically, without your approval. If you don't select this option, LinkedIn sends you a message whenever someone requests to join your group, and you must approve the request manually. This requires extra effort on your part, but it helps you ensure that only qualified people join your group.

12. If your group is for members who are located in a specific geographic location, select the Location check box. The Country and Postal Code fields appear so you can specify the exact location of your group.

13. Select a Language for your group. English is the default language for groups, but LinkedIn offers numerous language choices.

14. If you agree to the Terms of Service, select the Agreement check box. The Terms of Service cover your rights to provide LinkedIn with the email addresses of group members and LinkedIn's rights to use the logo you upload.

15. Click the Create Group button to create your group.

LinkedIn reviews your request to create a new group and approves the group if it meets LinkedIn guidelines.

Managing Your Group

After LinkedIn approves your group, you can start inviting and accepting members.

As a reminder, click the Groups link on the expanded left navigation menu to open the My Groups page where you can access all your LinkedIn groups. To manage your group, select the Manage tab on your group's page.

On the Manage tab, you can

▶ Approve or reject requests to join your group.

▶ Send invitations to LinkedIn members asking them to join your group.

▶ Upload a pre-approved list of email addresses for your group in the CSV format. This option is useful if your group also exists outside of LinkedIn, and you know the members you want to pre-approve.

TIP: **Create Your CSV File in Microsoft Excel**

Enter your list of pre-approved members in an Excel file with columns for First Name, Last Name, and Email. Save your spreadsheet as a CSV file. CSV stands for Comma Separated Values, a common text file format.

Summary

In this lesson, you learned how to join and participate in LinkedIn Groups, create your own groups, and manage your own groups.

Using LinkedIn Answers

In this lesson, you'll learn how to ask and answer questions that give you valuable feedback from the LinkedIn community and develop your reputation as an expert in your field.

Understanding LinkedIn Answers

LinkedIn Answers is an interactive feature that enables you to ask questions, receive input from a worldwide network of peers and experts, share your own expertise, and develop your platform as an expert.

CAUTION: **LinkedIn Answers Is for Professional Discussion, Not Promotion**

Understand that LinkedIn Answers is for genuine information sharing among professional peers. It's not the place for sales pitches (overt or disguised), open requests for help in getting a job, and so forth. That said, asking intelligent, relevant questions and providing useful answers with real value can help develop your expert image on LinkedIn.

To view questions and answers, click the Answers link on the top navigation menu. The Answers page opens, shown in Figure 12.1.

On the Answers Home tab, you can view the following:

▶ A box with shortcuts for asking and answering questions. LinkedIn recommends five categories based on previous questions you've answered. If you haven't answered questions, this section displays the Answer Now button.

▶ A list of recent questions from your network.

▶ The week's top experts, based on the number of questions they've answered and the number of times their answers have been selected as best answers.

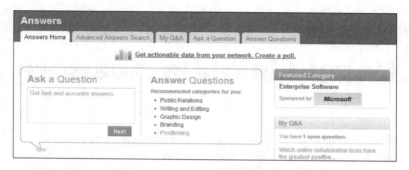

FIGURE 12.1   Participate in the LinkedIn community by asking and answering questions.

> ▶ The My Q&A box listing your open questions, if any.

> ▶ A complete list of LinkedIn Answers categories.

> ▶ Links to questions in French, Spanish, German, and English.

You can ask and answer questions that relate to professional topics in more than 20 categories, including Management, Marketing and Sales, Professional Development, Finance and Accounting, Technology, and more.

Your activity on LinkedIn Answers also appears in the Q & A box on your profile, shown in Figure 12.2.

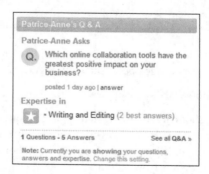

FIGURE 12.2   Your profile promotes your activity on LinkedIn Answers.

This box lists your questions, answers, and expertise. If you've received any best-answer votes, a green square with a white star appears in this box. To remove the Q&A box from your profile, click the Change This Setting link. For example, if you answer questions that don't relate to your professional experience, you might not want to display these on your profile.

Asking a Question

LinkedIn members with at least five connections can ask as many as 10 questions a month on LinkedIn Answers. LinkedIn imposes a limit to avoid the problem of "question spam" and to encourage members to ask questions of value to the LinkedIn community.

To ask a question:

1. Click the Answers link on LinkedIn's top navigation menu.

2. Click the Ask a Question tab to open the Ask a Question page. Figure 12.3 shows the Ask a Question page.

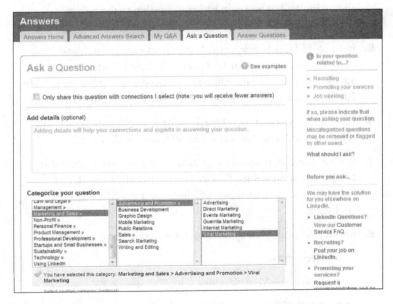

FIGURE 12.3 Ask a question and tap into the insight of LinkedIn's user base of 40 million members.

TIP: **Take a Shortcut in Asking a Question**
You can also ask your question in the Ask a Question box on the LinkedIn Answers Home tab. When you click Next, LinkedIn takes you to the Ask a Question tab where you can complete your question.

3. In the first text box, enter a one-line question. Make sure your question is clear and concise. Vague, open-ended questions rarely receive good feedback. For example, asking LinkedIn members for suggestions on online invoicing applications suited to a small business is a good, focused question. Asking members how to make lots of money with your new website, which you promote in the details section, is not the way to use LinkedIn Answers.

4. If you want to send your question only to specific people (up to 200 of your connections), select the Only Share This Question with Connections I Select check box. For maximum response and visibility, it's best to post your question to the public LinkedIn Answers section.

5. In the Add Details box, provide pertinent background information to clarify your question further. Be careful, however, of adding too much detail. Although you can add content up to 2,000 characters, many people skip over very lengthy questions.

6. Categorize your question based on the available categories and subcategories. You can add a second category if desired.

7. If your question is location-specific, select the My Question Is Focused Around a Specific Geographic Location check box. LinkedIn asks you to select a Country and Postal Code, if applicable.

8. Specify whether your question relates to one of the following:

   ▶ Recruiting

   ▶ Promoting Your Services

   ▶ Job Seeking

> NOTE: **Alternatives to LinkedIn Answers**
>
> If your question relates to recruiting, promotion, or a job search, LinkedIn offers links to other features that might be more appropriate than LinkedIn Answers. For example, consider posting a job using LinkedIn Jobs or promoting your services in LinkedIn Service Providers directory instead.

9. Click the Ask Question button to post your question.

LinkedIn's 40 million members now have the opportunity to view and answer your question, providing valuable feedback and information.

LinkedIn automatically closes your question in seven days, but offers you the choice to extend the question another week or close it manually before seven days. See the section "Viewing and Modifying Your Questions and Answers" later in this lesson for more information.

One final step is to select a best answer to the question you posted, if you feel one response provided the most value. LinkedIn members who receive the best answer designations are recognized in the LinkedIn Answers list of experts and on their profiles.

Browsing Open Questions to Answer

In addition to viewing questions to answer on the Answers Home tab, you can find more questions on the Answer Questions tab. When you select this tab, the Browse Open Questions page opens. Question summaries appear in the order of their author's connection to you. For example, questions from your 1st degree connections appear first, and so forth. Click the Date link to sort questions by date instead.

> TIP: **Answer Questions in LinkedIn's Recommended Categories**
>
> On the Answers Home tab, LinkedIn recommends question categories for you based on your profile and any questions you've previously answered.

Figure 12.4 shows a sample question summary.

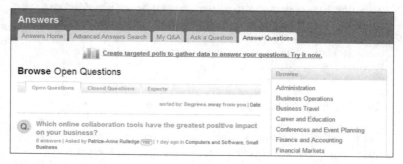

FIGURE 12.4   To elicit the best responses, ask clear, concise questions.

In addition to the question title, LinkedIn displays the number of answers the question has received, its author, the date it was posted, and its categories.

To browse questions relating to a specific category, click one of the links in the Browse box on the right side of your screen. Most categories have subcategories you can use to narrow the subject matter of posted questions.

TIP: **Subscribe to an RSS Feed to Stay Informed**

If you're interested in questions related to a specific category, you can subscribe to the RSS feed for that category. To do so, click the link next to the orange and white feed icon at the bottom of the Browse box. LinkedIn opens the Subscribe Now pop-up box, which enables you to subscribe using your favorite feed reader (such as My Yahoo!, Google, or Bloglines). See Lesson 4, "Customizing Your LinkedIn Settings," for more information about subscribing to RSS feeds.

You can also browse questions in a specific language. LinkedIn enables members to post questions in English, French, Spanish, and German.

Finally, the Browse Open Questions page also offers links for viewing closed questions and popular experts.

> NOTE: **Flagging Problem Questions**
>
> If you view a question that you feel is inappropriate, click the Flag Question As link below to question to alert LinkedIn staff. Potential reasons for flagging a question include duplicate questions, open advertising, recruitment messages, inappropriate content, connection-building spam, or misrepresentation.

Answering Questions

To post a public reply to a question, follow these steps:

1. Click the question title link to view the question's details. Figure 12.5 illustrates a sample question.

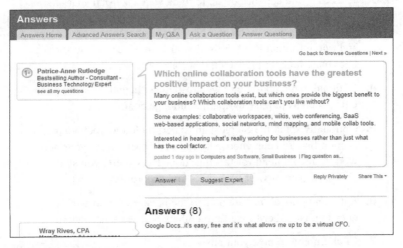

FIGURE 12.5   You can answer questions publicly or privately.

2. Click the Answer button to expand the Your Answer box, shown in Figure 12.6.

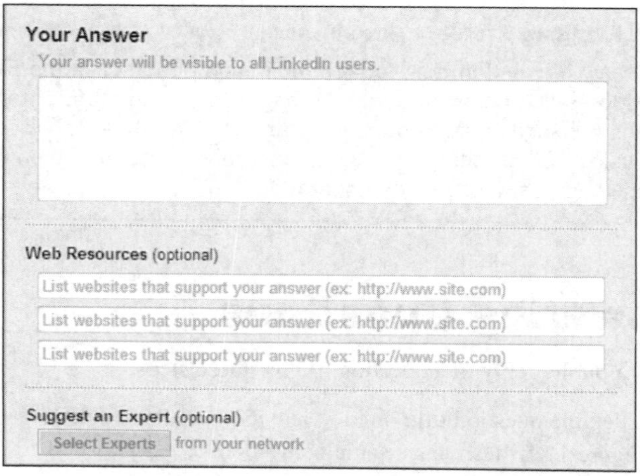

Your Answer

Your answer will be visible to all LinkedIn users.

Web Resources (optional)

List websites that support your answer (ex: http://www.site.com)

List websites that support your answer (ex: http://www.site.com)

List websites that support your answer (ex: http://www.site.com)

Suggest an Expert (optional)

Select Experts   from your network

FIGURE 12.6   You can include up to three web links with your answer.

3. Enter your answer in the text box. Remember to provide value and true information. Don't sell your own expertise and services. Let your LinkedIn profile do that for you.

4. Optionally, list up to three web resources. Include the complete URL, such as http://www.patricerutledge.com.

5. Optionally, click the Suggest an Expert button to open your connection list. You can choose up to three experts from your network to recommend for this question. The experts you suggest appear in your answer with links to their profiles.

6. Enter an optional, private note to the person who posted the question. No other LinkedIn members will see this content.

7. Click Submit to post your answer.

If you don't want to answer a question directly, you can

▶ Click the Suggest Expert button to choose expert referrals from your list of connections.

▶ Click the Reply Privately link to send a private message to the person who posted the question.

▶ Click the Share This link to email this question to others or post to the social bookmarking sites Delicious or Digg. This is a good way to expand the visibility of LinkedIn questions.

When you answer a question, it's important to provide an intelligent, helpful response. Responding to numerous questions with vague answers in an effort to increase your visibility won't pay off in the long run. Focus on quality rather than quantity and answer only when you have something meaningful to contribute.

LinkedIn members who post questions can award a best-answer designation to the person who provides the most helpful answer. When you receive Best Answer votes, you increase your ranking on the list of experts.

Searching LinkedIn Answers by Keyword

LinkedIn's advanced search functionality lets you search its vast collection of questions and answers for specific information.

Searching by keyword enables you to

▶ Find specific questions to answer

▶ Discover solutions to your own professional questions from LinkedIn's large collection of information

▶ Determine what people are asking and saying about you, your company, or your products

▶ Perform competitive intelligence

To search by keyword:

1. Click the Advanced Answers Search tab on the Answers page. Figure 12.7 shows your search possibilities.

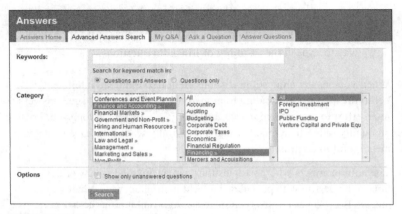

FIGURE 12.7 Search LinkedIn Answers for specific keywords.

2. In the Keywords field, enter your search terms. The more specific your keywords, the more targeted your results will be.

> TIP: **Take Advantage of Advanced Search Techniques**
> To search on a specific phrase, use quotation marks (such as "social media" to search specifically for social media). See Lesson 7, "Searching on LinkedIn," for more information about advanced searching techniques.

3. Specify whether you want to search in Questions and Answers or Questions Only.

4. Select a category and related subcategory in the Category field.

5. If you want to view only questions that haven't been answered, select the Show Only Unanswered Questions check box.

6. Click the Search button to display search results.

To view only open questions, click the Open Questions tab. From this page, you can also further refine your search criteria if necessary.

TIP: **Search LinkedIn Answers from the Quick Search Box**

You can also search LinkedIn Answers from the quick search box on LinkedIn's top navigation menu. Select Search Answers, enter your keywords, and click the Search button. Or click the Advanced Link to open the Advanced Answers Search tab.

Viewing and Modifying Your Questions and Answers

To view and modify your own activity on LinkedIn Answers, click the My Q&A tab on the Answers page.

On the first tab, My Questions, LinkedIn displays a summary of the questions you've asked. Click the link of any question to view it; if the questions is still open, you can revise it. Figure 12.8 shows a sample open question.

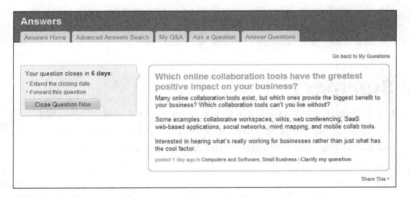

FIGURE 12.8   You can modify a question that's still open.

If the question is still open, you can

▶ Click the Extend the Closing Date link to extend the closing date by seven days.

- ► Click the Forward This Question link to send the question to up to 200 of your connections.

- ► Click the Close Question Now button to close the question before it closes automatically in seven days. You can also hide your closed question from public view. For maximum visibility, it's best to keep your question open and allow it to remain on LinkedIn Answers. If you make a mistake or no longer want to display your question, however, you can close and hide it.

- ► Click the Clarify My Question link, below the question itself, to open the Clarify Your Question page and add related details. LinkedIn doesn't allow you to edit the question you posted.

On the second tab, My Answers, LinkedIn displays summaries of all the questions you've answered. The right side of this page lists the categories in which you've demonstrated expertise (based on receiving "best answer" ratings), your answer ratings for closed questions, and statistics about your activity on LinkedIn Answers.

You can modify or delete your answers to open questions only. Click the Clarify My Answer link to add clarification to your existing answer. Click the Delete My Answer link to delete your answer.

Summary

In this lesson, you learned how to maximize the potential of LinkedIn Answers for finding professional solutions, demonstrating your expertise, and interacting with a worldwide audience of 40 million peers.

LESSON 13
Using LinkedIn Applications

In this lesson, you'll learn how to enhance your LinkedIn experience with LinkedIn applications, including how to add, manage, and remove these applications.

Understanding LinkedIn Applications

LinkedIn Applications are optional extensions to LinkedIn that enhance the content and effectiveness of your profile, foster collaboration with your network, and integrate your LinkedIn data with other sites to provide further research and competitive intelligence opportunities.

The following LinkedIn applications are currently available, with more in development:

- ▶ Blog Link by SixApart
- ▶ Box.net Files by Box.net
- ▶ Company Buzz by LinkedIn
- ▶ Google Presentation by Google
- ▶ Huddle Workspaces by Huddle.net
- ▶ My Travel by TripIt
- ▶ Polls by LinkedIn
- ▶ Reading List by Amazon
- ▶ SlideShare Presentations by SlideShare
- ▶ WordPress by WordPress

All LinkedIn applications are free, but some require you to have an account with an application that might charge fees based on your usage. For example, Box.net Files and Huddle Workspaces offer both free and fee-based plans.

Choosing the Right Applications

LinkedIn applications offer many options for sharing and collaborating. At times, the number of choices is overwhelming. Although some applications, such as My Travel and Company Buzz, are unique in terms of the features they provide, other applications overlap in their functionality. For example, both Blog Link and WordPress enable you to share blog posts on your profile. You can share presentations using Google Presentation, SlideShare Presentations, and even Box.net Files.

Here are some tips for making the most of LinkedIn applications:

- ▶ Analyze how each application fits into your strategic plan and helps you meet your goals. Just because something sounds interesting doesn't make it worthwhile to add.

- ▶ If more than one application performs the same function, compare their features before you pick one to use. Fortunately, LinkedIn applications are easy to add and remove.

- ▶ Focus on quality rather than quantity when choosing the documents and presentations you would like to share. A resume, portfolio, or presentation that highlights your business can enhance the effectiveness and reach of your LinkedIn profile, but don't add so many documents that the important ones are lost in the mix.

- ▶ Consider your personal privacy with all the documents and data you share online. For example, adding your resume to your profile can aid in your job search, but you might not want to include your home address or phone number.

- ▶ Determine whether you have the legal right to post presentations or other documents you created for an employer.

Adding Applications

To add an application to your profile or home page, follow these steps:

1. Click the Applications link on the left navigation menu, or click the Add Application link on the Edit My Profile page. The Featured Applications page opens (see Figure 13.1).

FIGURE 13.1 Enhance your LinkedIn experience with one of the many available applications.

2. Select the application you want to add. The page for that application opens. Figure 13.2 illustrates the Google Presentation page, as an example.

3. The Application Info box appears on the right side of every application page. In this box, choose whether you want to display the application on your profile or on your LinkedIn home page.

4. Click the Add Application button to add the application and enter details specific to that application.

The rest of this section explains how to set up individual applications. This lesson provides detailed instructions for only the most popular applications, not every available application.

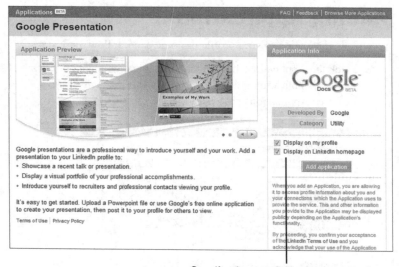

Specify where to display your application

FIGURE 13.2   Google Presentation is one of many LinkedIn applications.

When you add an application, a link to it appears below the Applications link on the expanded left navigation menu. If you haven't added any applications, only the Reading List by Amazon and Events links appear by default.

NOTE: **You Can Also Add Applications from Your Profile**

You can also add applications from the Edit My Profile page. Click the Edit My Profile link on the expanded left navigation menu to open this page. Scroll down to the Applications section, and click the Add Application link to open the Featured Applications page. Applications you add will appear in this section if you choose to display them on your profile.

Adding the Blog Link Application

The Blog Link application enables you to post summaries of your blog posts to your LinkedIn profile. You can also follow the blog posts of LinkedIn members in your network. Blog Link supports blogs on multiple platforms including TypePad, Movable Type, Vox, Wordpress.com, Wordpress.org, Tumblr, Blogger, LiveJournal, and more.

NOTE: **If You Use WordPress, Consider the WordPress Application**

WordPress users have two choices for displaying their blog posts on their profile: the Blog Link application and the WordPress application. Both applications serve the same function, but they display your blog posts in a different format. If you use WordPress, try both applications to see which one you prefer. See "Adding the WordPress Application," later in this lesson for more information.

Before adding the Blog Link application, verify that the URL to your blog appears in the Websites section on your profile. See Lesson 2, "Creating Your Profile," for more information on listing your blog in this section. The application pulls your blog data from your profile and doesn't work properly if you don't have a listed blog.

To add the Blog Link application, follow the steps listed in "Adding Applications" earlier in this lesson, selecting the Blog Link application on the Featured Applications page. The Blog Link application opens.

The Blog Link application searches for your blog posts and includes summaries on your LinkedIn profile (see Figure 13.3). They also appear on the From Me tab in the Blog Link application.

FIGURE 13.3   Automatically post your blog updates to your LinkedIn profile.

> CAUTION: **What to Do if Your Blog Posts Don't Appear on Your Profile**
>
> If your blog posts don't appear on your profile, verify that you selected the Display on My Profile check box on the initial application page. Also, verify that your blog is listed on the Websites section of your profile. The Blog Link application pulls its content from the blog listed in this section.

Blog Link also searches for blog posts from your connections and includes these on the From My Contacts tab. If you don't want to view a particular blog, click the Hide This Feed link below its title. Blog posts from other LinkedIn members don't appear on your profile.

> CAUTION: **Only Add Blogs That Relate to Your Professional Activities**
>
> Remember that your LinkedIn profile is part of your professional presence online. Include only blog content that supports your professional image. Personal blogs or blogs covering controversial topics might not be suitable to share with your LinkedIn connections.

Adding the Box.net Files Application

The Box.net Files application enables you to share content from Box.net (www.box.net), a leading online collaboration and file-sharing website. With this application, you can post files such as resumes, portfolios, and presentations to your profile, collaborate privately with your LinkedIn connections, and view and edit your files online.

To add the Box.net Files application, follow the steps listed in the "Adding Applications" section earlier in this lesson, selecting the Box.net Files application on the Featured Applications page.

The Box.net Files application opens, requesting that you log in to your Box.net Files account or sign up for a free account.

After you log in, you can upload files, view your connections' public files, and collaborate privately with your connections.

The files you selected to display publicly on your profile appear in the Applications section, shown in Figure 13.4.

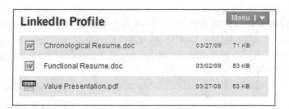

FIGURE 13.4 Posting your resume can help job seekers stand out from the crowd.

Adding a Poll

The Polls application enables you to poll LinkedIn users about relevant professional topics. A LinkedIn poll is a short question with the option of providing as many as five answers. Members select their preferred answer and the Polls application tallies the results. Polls are different from other applications in that they don't integrate with external data and they offer both free and fee-based options.

You can invite your 1st degree connections on LinkedIn to participate in your poll at no charge or purchase a paid poll that surveys a wider audience on LinkedIn. If you choose to purchase a paid poll, you can specify a target audience based on job function, seniority, gender, age, or geography. You pay a set fee of $1 per response with a minimum purchase of 50 responses. If you're a LinkedIn premium member, you might be eligible for discounts or special offers.

To create a poll, follow these steps:

1. Follow the steps listed in the "Adding Applications" section earlier in this lesson, selecting the Polls application on the Featured Applications page. The Create a Poll page opens, shown in Figure 13.5.

2. Enter a Question of no more than 75 characters.

3. Enter up to five possible answers (using no more than 30 characters per answer) to your question.

> TIP: **Review the Poll Preview Box for Accuracy**
>
> Review the Poll Preview box to ensure that your poll is accurate. You can't edit it after submitting, so be careful to avoid spelling, grammar, or content errors.

4. Click the Rotate the Order of the Answers check box if you want to vary the position of your answers in your poll.

5. Select the Audience for your poll's distribution. Options include

> ▶ **Target Audience of Professionals in the U.S**. With this option, you can select a target audience and receive a guaranteed response for a fee.

> ▶ **Your 1st Degree Connections**. LinkedIn sends a network update informing your connections about your poll. The number of responses you receive will vary based on your number of connections and their interest in participating in your poll. LinkedIn will also provide you with a URL you can use to share your poll with others.

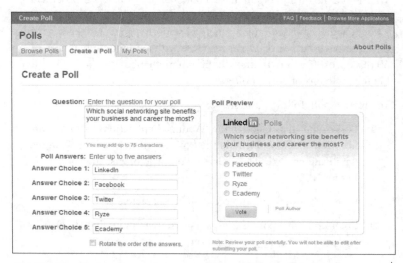

FIGURE 13.5   Use a LinkedIn poll to gain valuable insight and perform market research.

6. Click the Post Poll button to post your poll to the Network Updates section on your connections' home page. If you selected the fee-based poll option, LinkedIn opens additional pages for you to specify your target audience and pay for your poll before posting.

To view the results of your polls, click the My Polls tab on the Polls page. On this tab, you can select a poll to view, copy a poll for reuse, or end a poll.

When you click the title link of a poll, LinkedIn displays detailed information about your poll in the Poll Results section, shown in Figure 13.6.

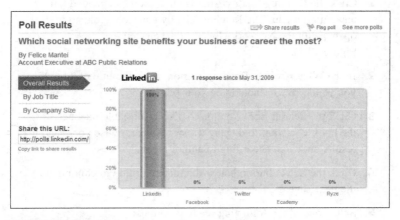

FIGURE 13.6   Analyze the results of your poll.

Here you can

▶ View the total number of responses you've received. Note that each LinkedIn member can vote only once, so no one can skew poll results.

- ► View the response percentage for each potential answer.

- ► View responses by job title and company size.

- ► Share your poll's unique URL with others.

- ► Add and review comments.

To view and respond to polls other LinkedIn members submit, click the Browse Polls tab.

Adding the Reading List by Amazon Application

The Reading List by Amazon application enables you to share book recommendations and reading plans with your LinkedIn connections. This application appears by default on the expanded left navigation menu.

To use the Reading List by Amazon application, follow these steps:

1. Click the Reading List by Amazon link on the expanded left navigation menu. The Reading List by Amazon application opens, with the Network Updates tab selected (see Figure 13.7).

2. In the What Are You Reading section, enter the title of a book you would like to include on your profile.

3. Click the Search Books button to display possible matches. If the book you want to display doesn't appear, revise your search results or search according to author name.

4. Click the Select button below the matching title to continue to the next page.

5. Select one of the following reading options:

- ► I Want to Read It

- ► I'm Reading It Now

- ► I Read It

Enter book name here

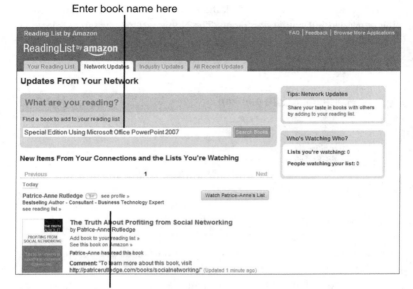

See what your connections are reading

FIGURE 13.7 Share your reading recommendations with your network.

TIP: **Recommend Books to Your Connections**

If you select the I Read It option button, the I Recommend This Book check box appears. Select this check box if you want to recommend this book to your connections.

---

6. Enter a comment of up to 5,000 characters. In your comments, explain to your connections why you're including this book and the value it offers.

7. Select the I'm Reading This Book on My Kindle check box if you're reading the Kindle version.

8. Click the Save button to update your reading list.

The book now appears on your profile (see Figure 13.8) and home page (if you selected these display options).

To return to this application, click the Reading List by Amazon link on the expanded left navigation menu. The Network Updates tab is selected by default.

FIGURE 13.8   Your connections can view your reading list on your profile.

This tab also includes information about the books your connections are reading. For each book that appears, you can click the

▶ Title of the book for more information about the book

▶ See Profile link to view the profile of the person who recommends this book

▶ Watch [First Name]'s List button to add yourself to this person's watch list

▶ Add Book to Your Reading List link to add the book to your own reading list

▶ See This Book on Amazon link to open the book's Amazon page

In addition to the Network Updates tab, the Reading List by Amazon application also includes three other tabs:

▶ **Your Reading List**. Displays a list of all books you added to your reading list. You can edit or delete an existing entry from this list.

▶ **Industry Updates**. Displays books on the reading lists of others in your industry.

- ▶ **All Recent Updates**. Displays reading list updates from all LinkedIn members.

If you remove the Reading List by Amazon application and want to add it again, follow the steps listed in the "Adding Applications" section earlier in this lesson.

Adding the SlideShare Presentations Application

Using the SlideShare Presentations application, you can embed presentations and other documents from SlideShare (www.slideshare.net), the popular presentation-sharing site. If you don't have an account on SlideShare, you can sign up for one from LinkedIn and start uploading files. The files you choose appear on your profile.

Although SlideShare is best known for sharing presentations such as PowerPoint files, you can also share files of up to 100MB in numerous formats, including Microsoft Word, Microsoft Excel, and PDF. You can also embed YouTube videos in your presentations to give your LinkedIn profile some added flair.

To add the SlideShare Presentations application, follow the steps listed in the "Adding Applications" section earlier in this lesson, selecting the SlideShare Presentations application on the Featured Applications page. The SlideShare application opens.

Enter your Username and Password if you already have a SlideShare account and click the Link Existing Profile button. Alternatively, sign up for a SlideShare account and click the Create New Profile button.

The SlideShare application includes the following four tabs, shown in Figure 13.9:

- ▶ **Home**. Displays the Network Activity list, detailing the presentations your connections have uploaded. Click the name of any presentation to view it in a player, tweet it on Twitter, share with your connections, add comments, or mark it as a favorite.

- ▶ **Explore**. Lists the most viewed and most recently uploaded presentations.

▶ **Your Slidespace**. Offers the following display options: Your Presentations, Your Favorites, or Your Connections. This tab also includes a link to the Settings page where you can specify whether you want to display presentation thumbnails or a complete presentation in a player.

▶ **Upload**. Enables you to upload files to LinkedIn.

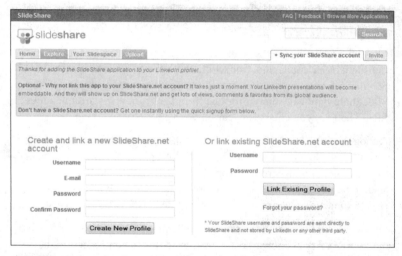

FIGURE 13.9   Use SlideShare to incorporate slideshows into your LinkedIn profile.

Adding the WordPress Application

If you have a WordPress blog, you can display your blog posts on your LinkedIn profile. This application works with both self-hosted WordPress.org blogs and hosted WordPress.com blogs.

TIP: **Also Consider the Blog Link Application**

If you use a solution other than WordPress to host your blog, check out the Blog Link application instead. WordPress users can choose between adding the WordPress application or adding the Blog Link application. Each application performs the same function, but each displays posts in different formats. See the "Adding the Blog Link Application" section earlier in this lesson for more information.

To add the WordPress application, follow these steps:

1. Follow the steps listed in the "Adding Applications" section earlier in this lesson, selecting the WordPress application on the Featured Applications page. The WordPress application opens, shown in Figure 13.10.

FIGURE 13.10 Specify the URL of your WordPress blog.

2. Enter the complete URL of your blog in the text box, such as http://www.patricerutledge.com/blog.

3. Indicate whether you want to show all recent blog posts or only those tagged LinkedIn.

TIP: **You Can Choose to Include Only Selected Blog Posts on LinkedIn**

Tag your blog posts in WordPress with the "linkedin" tag to select which ones you want to appear on LinkedIn.

4. Click the Save button to preview your blog posts.

Your WordPress blog posts now appear on your profile (see Figure 13.11) and home page (if you selected these display options).

FIGURE 13.11   View your blog posts on your LinkedIn profile.

Adding and Managing LinkedIn Events

The LinkedIn Events feature enables you to add events to LinkedIn's events calendar, promote events to LinkedIn members, and find events you want to attend. LinkedIn focuses on professional events, both in-person and virtual, rather than personal events.

Although the Events link appears in the Applications section on the expanded left navigation menu, events differ from other LinkedIn applications. First, there is no actual application to add. Second, the Events link appears by default on this menu even if you haven't added any application.

To open the LinkedIn Events page, click the Events link on the expanded left navigation menu. This page contains four tabs:

- ▶ **Events Home**. Browse your connections' events, the most popular events on LinkedIn, and event-related network updates. Click an event's title link to view more details, add comments, and RSVP your participation at the event (such as attending, presenting, exhibiting, or interested). This isn't an official RSVP, but rather a way to let your LinkedIn network know about your event activities. You can also see how many other LinkedIn members RSVPed, including your connections.

- ▶ **Find Events**. Search for events to attend by keyword, date, location, or event type. Figure 13.12 shows a sample Search Results summary, which also lets you know about your connections' participation.

Find connections who are attending   RSVP your status

FIGURE 13.12   Use LinkedIn Events to find events to attend and share with your network.

- ▶ **My Events**. View a list of the events you added or those events for which you submitted an RSVP.

- ▶ **Add an Event**. Add your own events to the LinkedIn events calendar. Figure 13.13 shows a sample new event.

LinkedIn provides event visibility in its event directory, on member home pages, and member profiles. You can also send a message to your connections about a particular event by clicking the Share link on that event's page. Advertising via LinkedIn DirectAds is another way to promote your event. See Web Lesson 3, "Advertising on LinkedIn," for more information about placing DirectAds.

FIGURE 13.13   Add an event and publicize it on LinkedIn.

Removing Applications

Eventually, you might discover that an application isn't as useful as you thought it would be and you want to remove it:

1. Click the Applications link on the left navigation menu.

2. On the Featured Applications page, click the link for the application you want to remove.

3. In the Application Info box on the right side of the page, click the Remove button.

LinkedIn removes the application from your profile and home page.

You can also update an application's visibility settings from this page. For example, rather than removing an application, you could choose not to display it on your profile or LinkedIn home page.

Summary

In this lesson, you learned how to use LinkedIn applications to enhance your profile and collaborate with your connections.

Using LinkedIn Service Providers

In this lesson, you'll learn how to locate recommended service providers in the LinkedIn Service Providers directory, make your own recommendations, and request recommendations if you provide professional services.

Understanding LinkedIn Service Providers

The LinkedIn Service Providers feature connects members searching for service providers with members who provide services. If you're searching for a service provider, you can review peer recommendations before hiring. If you provide professional services, you can receive client recommendations and promote your services to prospective buyers through the LinkedIn database of service providers.

> CAUTION: **Understand the Difference Between Recommendation Types**
>
> If you're not a service provider, ask for a colleague or business partner recommendation rather than a service provider recommendation. See Lesson 10, "Requesting and Providing Recommendations," for more information.

LinkedIn offers numerous categories and subcategories of service providers such as Consulting, Employment Services, Financial & Legal Services, and Health & Medical.

Searching for Service Providers

Finding the right service provider is a straightforward process. Click the down arrow to the right of the Companies link on the top navigation menu, and select Service Providers from the drop-down list. Figure 14.1 illustrates the Service Provider Recommendations page.

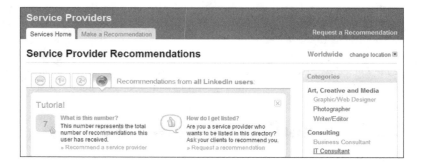

FIGURE 14.1   Learn about the service providers your fellow LinkedIn members recommend.

By default, LinkedIn lists summaries of the most recent recommendations from all members, but you can click the buttons at the top of the page to modify what appears. Options include displaying only your own recommendations, displaying recommendations from 1st degree connections, or displaying recommendations from 2nd degree connections.

> TIP: **Evaluate Recommendations Carefully Before Making Decisions**
>
> Although the LinkedIn Service Providers directory can help you find quality professionals to perform specialized tasks, it's important to analyze recommendations before making a hiring decision. Who are the people making the recommendations? Do the recommendations include valid insight into the provider's performance, or are they vague compliments? How many recommendations does a particular provider have? In many cases, the quantity of recommendations is less important than the quality of recommendations.

To search for a specific type of service provider, click the appropriate service category in the Categories box on the right side of the page. LinkedIn narrows the results on the Service Providers page to providers only in that category.

If you want to find providers who live in your local area, click the Change Location link. Select a Country and optional Postal Code and click the Change Location button to view providers in that geographic area. Alternatively, you can choose one of the Top Locations for service providers.

Recommending a Service Provider

To recommend a LinkedIn member who did an outstanding job performing a professional service, follow these steps:

1. On the top LinkedIn navigation menu, click the down arrow to the right of the Companies link and select Service Providers from the drop-down list.

2. Select the Make a Recommendation tab.

3. Click the Select from Your Connection List link to open your connection list in another window.

4. Select the person you want to recommend. LinkedIn returns to the Make a Recommendation tab.

NOTE: **Recommending Someone Who's Not Your Connection**

If you're not connected to the person you want to recommend, enter that person's name and email address. You can even recommend a provider who isn't a LinkedIn member.

---

5. Click the Continue button. LinkedIn opens the Create Your Recommendation page, shown in Figure 14.3.

6. Select the position you're recommending the person for from the drop-down list. This should be the position associated with the service provider's business.

7. Select a Service Category from the drop-down list.

8. In the Year First Hired field, indicate when you first start working with this service provider.

9. If you've worked with this person before, select the I Have Hired [First Name] More than Once check box.

10. Select up to three attributes for this service provider. LinkedIn allows you to choose only three, so consider carefully which are the most applicable.

11. Enter your recommendation in the text box. Provide specific, concise reasons why you're recommending this person. Vague accolades or short comments like "great guy" don't make effective recommendations. Instead, focus on actual accomplishments

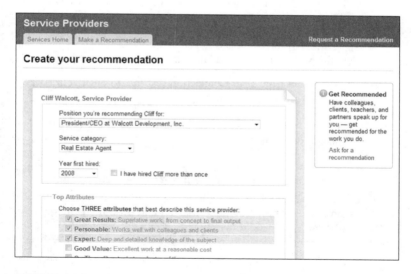

FIGURE 14.3 Recommend top service providers so others can find them in LinkedIn's Service Provider directory.

and quantifiable achievements. For example, "Ken consistently ranked as one of our top five sales representatives" or "Samantha's marketing campaign increased our website traffic by 25 percent."

12. Click the Send button to send a notification message to the provider that you recommend.

In this message, shown in Figure 14.4, the provider can accept the recommendation, request a replacement recommendation, or archive the recommendation for future consideration.

Providers also have the choice to display or hide your recommendation on their profile. Figure 14.5 shows a provider profile recommendation.

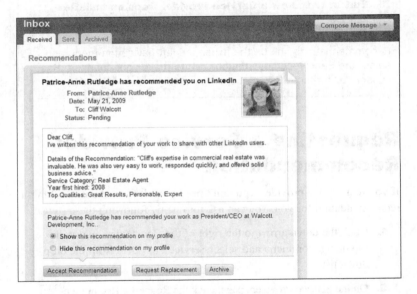

FIGURE 14.4   Providers have the option of accepting or asking for changes on any recommendation they receive.

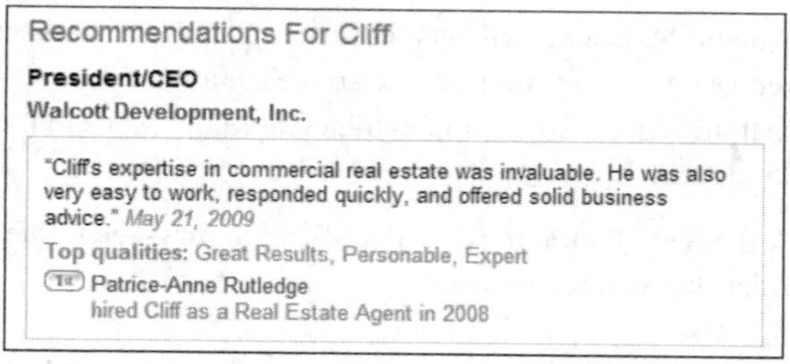

Recommendations For Cliff

President/CEO
Walcott Development, Inc.

"Cliff's expertise in commercial real estate was invaluable. He was also very easy to work, responded quickly, and offered solid business advice." *May 21, 2009*

Top qualities: Great Results, Personable, Expert

Patrice-Anne Rutledge
    hired Cliff as a Real Estate Agent in 2008

FIGURE 14.5   Providers can display recommendations for their connections—and potential clients—to see.

TIP: **Edit or Withdraw a Service Provider Recommendation**

You can edit or withdraw (delete) a service provider recommendation just as you can any other recommendation. Click the Recommendations link on the expanded left navigation menu and select the Sent Recommendations tab to make your changes. See Lesson 10 for more information.

Requesting a Service Provider Recommendation

If you're a service provider, you don't need to wait for a client to submit a recommendation for you. You can ask for one by following these steps:

1. Click the down arrow to the right of the Companies link on the top navigation menu and select Service Providers from the drop-down list.

2. On the Service Providers page, click the Request a Recommendation link. Figure 14.6 shows the Request Recommendations page.

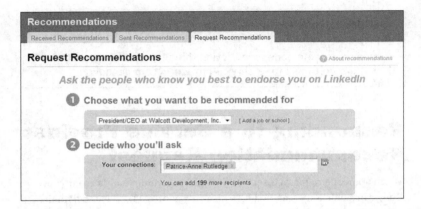

FIGURE 14.6   Request a recommendation to gain visibility in the Service Providers directory.

3. In step 1, choose the position for which you want the recommendation from the drop-down list. This should be the job associated with your work as a service provider.

4. In step 2, select connections to ask for a recommendation. Click the View All Connections icon to select from a list of your connections. Although you can contact up to 200 connections, it's a much better practice to contact one person at a time and customize your request.

5. When you're finished selecting connections, click the Finished button to return to the Request Recommendations page.

6. In step 3, you can use the sample text LinkedIn provides or, preferably, replace it with a personalized message.

7. Click the Send button to send your recommendation request for completion and approval.

Read "Responding to a Service Provider Recommendation Request," later in this lesson to learn more about what happens after you send your request.

> TIP: **Specify That You Want a Service Provider Recommendation**
> Because a recommender can provide three types of recommendations, be sure to ask for a service provider recommendation.

Responding to a Service Provider Recommendation Request

When someone requests a service provider recommendation from you, LinkedIn sends a message with "Can You Endorse Me?" as the default subject line.

If you want to provide a recommendation, follow these steps:

1. Click the subject line to open the Recommendations page.

2. Click the Write Recommendations button to open the Select Type page.

3. Select Service Provider as the recommendation type you want to write.

4. Click the Continue button to open the Create Your Recommendation page. The fields on this page are the same whether you take the initiative to create a service provider recommendation or respond to a request for one. See "Recommending a Service Provider," earlier in this lesson for details about how to complete this page.

Summary

In this lesson, you learned how to find recommended service providers and how to receive recommendations if you provide professional services.

Index

F

K - L

O - P

open groups, 147

open networkers, 38

OpenLink Network, 7

Outlook Toolbar, 107, 115-116

passwords, changing, 65

people searches, 98-99
  advanced searches, 103-104
  narrowing results, 100-102
  saving searches, 105

personal information
  adding to profiles, 22
  customizing, 64-65

photos, profiles
  adding to, 34-35
  removing from, 36, 57
  uploading to, 57
  viewing in, 67

polls, 107, 183-186

positions, profiles
  adding to, 23-24
  focus of employment histories, 25
  removing from, 24

postings
  blog postings, 155-156
  job postings on discussion boards, 154, 158-159
  searching job postings, 122-126

Preferences option (Firefox Browser Toolbar), 110-112

premium accounts, 6-7

presentations, SlideShare Presentations application, 189-190

previewing profiles, 36

printing profiles, 78

privacy
  customizing, 66-67
  email addresses, 9
  group discussions, 154
  LinkedIn settings, customizing for, 55
  private feeds, 63
  profiles, 20, 33, 66

Pro Accounts, 7

Professional Headlines (profiles), 22

profiles
  adding applications, 179
  Basic Information page, 22
  Blog Link application, 180-182, 191
  Box.net Files application, 182
  completing, 20
  contact information, 32
  contact profiles, 52
  Contact Settings page, 33-34
  creating, 18-28, 34-35, 76-77
  customizing, 29-30, 56-57, 75
  display names, 22
  downloading, 78
  Edit My Profile page, 134
  educational information, 25-27
  employment histories, focus of, 25
  forwarding to connections, 83
  features of, 18
  former/maiden names, 22
  goals of, 18-19
  hiding, 30

Q - R

FREE Online Edition

Your purchase of **Sams Teach Yourself LinkedIn in 10 Minutes** includes access to a free online edition for 45 days through the Safari Books Online subscription service. Nearly every Sams book is available online through Safari Books Online, along with more than 5,000 other technical books and videos from publishers such as Addison-Wesley Professional, Cisco Press, Exam Cram, IBM Press, O'Reilly, Prentice Hall, and Que.

SAFARI BOOKS ONLINE allows you to search for a specific answer, cut and paste code, download chapters, and stay current with emerging technologies.

Activate your FREE Online Edition at www.informit.com/safarifree

> **STEP 1:** Enter the coupon code: YXCIPXA.

> **STEP 2:** New Safari users, complete the brief registration form. Safari subscribers, just log in.

If you have difficulty registering on Safari or accessing the online edition, please e-mail customer-service@safaribooksonline.com